# Fvck It

FVCK IT: A Soul's Rise To Life



Ascensus Press

ISBN: 979-8-9953623-0-2

First Edition

Scripture quotations are taken from the King James Version of the Holy Bible (KJV). Published by Thomas Nelson, a division of HarperCollins Christian Publishing, Inc., 2017.

Cover design: Annie Zastera

Printed in the United States of America

Legal Disclaimer:

This book is intended for informational, educational, inspirational, and spiritual reflection purposes only. It reflects the author's personal experiences, opinions, observations, beliefs, and creative expression. It is not medical, psychological, psychiatric, therapeutic, legal, tax, financial, or other professional advice, diagnosis, or treatment. Nothing in this

*Dedicated to:*
*God, the Father. My Savior Jesus Christ.*
*The Holy Spirit for their constant comfort and guidance, without whom this book would not have been possible.*

*My daughter.*

*My son.*

*My mother.*

*Emma.*

*In Loving Memory of my dad.*

# Fvck It

## The Soul's Rise To Life:

## A Faithful Framework For Purposeful Living

JONATHAN NOLAN

# Table of Contents

# Before The Walls Come Down...

You really don't need another self-help book.
And this really isn't one.

You may have already met the usual suspects on the "Personal Growth" shelf:

10 habits to become unstoppable.
7 steps to manifest your dream life.
14 ways to "just think positive"
13 things to think your way into becoming a millionaire.

Meanwhile, you're doom scrolling at 2 a.m., whispering something closer to:

"I can't keep going on like this. There's so much pressure on my shoulders and I don't even really know why. But I know my chest hurts whenever I walk into my office."

That statement, and anything similar to it, is why this book exists.

I didn't write this because my life is a highlight reel.
I wrote it because my life felt like crime scene after crime scene.

I've been the overachiever, the overthinker, the good church kid, the quiet kid, the kid who learned early that keeping the peace meant losing his voice.

I've swallowed my anger, weaponized my empathy, and tried to outrun my own history with productivity and perfection.

All while making sure everyone around me is happy and content.

I’m the atypical neurodivergent who was handed an array of typical masks at a very young age.

I’ve held my dying father in my arms.
I've watched friends lose their lives right in front of me.
I’ve watched the bottom drop out of my faith, my mental health, my plans, and my identity—more times than I care to count.

And in the middle of it all, God never handed me a cute little devotional and a scented candle. He didn’t provide anything I was asking for—anything I was praying for—in the way I wanted it.

He gutted me with His love and grace.

He tore up floors I thought were solid. He ripped out walls I wallpapered with “positive thinking.” He went after expectations, emotions, fear, shame, and the way I kept falling down.

“Fuck it” became my real prayer.

Not the apathetic, teenage-typical, “whatever” kind of apathy.

The most genuine kind of desperate surrender:

“Fuck it. God, I can’t pretend anymore. Take everything. Tear down what’s rotting. Build something true out of me. Build me on your Rock. Your will. Not mine.”

This book is the blueprint that came out of that surrender.

It's the book I needed when I was drowning under expectations; when my nervous system was wrecked, my emotions were running the show, and every fall felt like compounding evidence that I was broken beyond repair.

## God's Co-Author

This didn't fall out of the sky on a weekend of "inspiration." However, there was one BIG moment in 2018 that sparked it, which I need to put on the back burner to simmer—for now.

Everything you find in this book comes from:

Years of therapy and trauma work.

Countless all nighters with an open Bible, an open browser full of neuroscience studies, and journals.

Coaching conversations with people who were tired of being told to "just believe" and "be positive" while their bodies screamed "we're not safe."

A lot of journal pages, even more prayers, a wee bit of profanity, and so many tears the Hoover Dam would struggle to contain the flow.

A lifetime of being told he's the "too much" kid and the "not enough" man.

A spiritual battle with God Himself spanning well over a decade.

Piece by piece, God kept showing me the same patterns:

Expectations that crush instead of call.
Emotions that either run wild or get locked in the basement.
Fear that masquerades as wisdom.

Falling down was actually the training grounds, not a disqualification from the match.

I started naming the real issues the way we actually talk about them:

Fuck Expectations.
Fuck Emotions.
Fuck Fear.
Fuck Falling Down.

Not as a middle finger to God, but as a middle finger to the clever lies that keep us from Him.

The notes, journals, sermons, conversations, and scars turned into chapters. Those chapters turned into a path. And that path?

That path turned into this book.

## Who Needs To Skip A Couple Lattes

This book is for you if:

You love God (or want to), but you're allergic to religious bullshit.

You've done the devotionals, the vision boards, the affirmations, the manifesting, the meditating, but still feel stuck.

You're the black sheep, the overthinker, the "overly" sensitive one—the one who "feels too much."

You've been told to "stop swearing and just trust God," while no one helps you process the trauma burning holes in your chest.

You're tired of numbing yourself in any way—it's not only drugs and alcohol.

You're ready to stop treating your soul like a DIY Pinterest project and start letting God renovate it for real.

This is not a book for people who want a cute Christian bumper sticker to cover their pain.

It's for the ones curled up on the bathroom floor grieving life.

The ones who love Jesus and still feel haunted.

The ones angry with Jesus for where they are in life.

The ones who want to love Jesus, but need to learn to love themselves.

The ones who are one "fuck it" away from giving up—and need that same "fuck it" to become their doorway back to life.

## Why This Book Is Nothing Like The Self-Help Aisle

Most self-help books treat you like a system needing optimization.

Pointing out the obvious stuff:

Wake up earlier.
Hustle harder.
Think happier thoughts.
Manifest better outcomes.

This book assumes something more sacred and more brutal:
**You're not a brand; you're a soul.**

Souls don't need optimization.
They need renovation.
And I intend to deliver.

Instead of: "Here are 5 hacks to never feel fear again,"

You'll get: "Here's why God allows fear, how your brain and body respond to it, and how to walk through it with Him instead of pretending you don't feel it at all."

Instead of: "Just let go of expectations,"

You'll get: "Here's where your expectations came from, how they attached to your nervous system, how Scripture speaks into them, and how to dismantle the ones that are choking you."

Instead of: “Failure is feedback,”

You’ll get: “Here’s why you keep getting knocked down in the same places, how shame hijacks your story, and how God uses falling down as training, not proof that you’re disqualified.”

This book lives where Scripture, science, and real life sit together at the same table:

Neuroscience and psychology to explain what’s happening in your brain and body.

Biblical truth to anchor your identity and purpose.

Raw stories to remind you you’re not insane or alone.

No fluff.
No prosperity gospel shortcuts.
No spiritual gaslighting dressed up as “faith.”

Just holy ground and heavy lifting.

# A Note on Language (Why the Profanity and What I Did About It)

Let's talk about the elephant—and the F-word—in the room.

The title isn't an edgy marketing gimmick. The profanity throughout the body is not here to shock you for sport.

It's here because this is the language most of us actually use in the dark.

When your chest caves in. When the diagnosis hits. When the marriage crumbles. When the addiction wins again. When grief still ambushes you in the cereal aisle.

Most people don't say, "Well gosh, this is mildly inconvenient." Most say some version of, "Fuck. This again?!"

I refused to sanitize those moments for anyone's opinion.

Because God met me there, not in the pretend clean version of my vocabulary choices. He didn't wait for me to say it "nicely" before He showed up.

So in the original edition, the profanity stays:
Because it's honest.
Because it matches the intensity of the battle.
Because sometimes "fuck it" is the only bridge between your

breaking point and your surrender.

But I also understand this:
Some of you—and some communities, churches, families, schools—have real, practical or conscience-based barriers with that language due to calling, context, or conviction.

Maybe this book will be used in a group setting where the language would be a stumbling block. Or whatever other reason a person or group doesn't want the language.

I don't give a fuck about the reason but I respect it.

Both God and I care mucho more about the message transforming your life than I do about guarding my right to drop F-bombs on any page I want.

That's why there is a censored-language edition.

Same book. Same truth. Same renovation.

The boards, nails, Scripture, science, stories, and exercises are all still here.The only difference is the words used to carry the same message.

The original version mirrors the way many of us talk. Period.

The censored version mirrors the way some of us talk out loud in our communities.

Both are holy ground.
Choose whichever one lets you hear God more clearly.

# The Part Only Some Care About

**If you rather jump to the instructions for the book, feel free to skip ahead to the "Quick Start Guide."**

**But if you want some backstory behind the voice, just keep reading.**

**Much love to you either way...**

## Pooter Scooter

On January 26, 1986, during Super Bowl XX, Chicago Bears defensive lineman named William "The Refrigerator" Perry made history. Standing 6'2" with 335 pounds of pure locomotion, he took a handoff as a running back, and bulldozed his way into the end zone.

Four days later, on January 30th, I was born.

I came into the world at ten pounds of fresh humanity, with baby rolls reminiscent of the Stay Puft Marshmallow Man, and set of lungs full of purpose.

Legend has it, one of the doctors nicknamed me "The Freezer." A newborn to earn a nickname like that warms my heart. It reminds me I came into this world to make a heavy impact. The nickname didn't stick, but another did.

"Pooter Scooter" for some reason or another became the nickname of choice.

That one stuck. (Thanks, Dad!)

I rolled my eyes at it growing up, especially when I brought any girl over to meet them. But even the day I held my father for the last time he said, "Thanks for everything you did, Pooter."

Pooter (for short) began to serve as a reminder of having been in motion my whole life.

Forward motion.

Not because I never get knocked back—I do—but because I don't step backwards on my own.

Even when I don't know where I'm going.
Even when I can't see where my next step is.

I am moving forward, moving upward, moving through.

There are many names for it...
I'm going to call it divine momentum.

## The Warrior and the Mediator

Idle hands have led me into trouble here and there.
My. Body. Has. To. Move.

And so naturally, at a young age, I fell in love with athletics.

It wasn't just about the sport; it was the love of competition. It wasn't even really about winning, but this drive for excellence within myself.

"I can do better."
"I have more to give than this."
"Kaizen" might as well be my middle name.
An incessant drive to always get better.

**A "becoming."**

Sharper. Stronger. Steadier.

At a young age, I realized God wasn't trying to make me "better" than anyone else. He was making me better for myself.

That's how the forge of life works: He melts the impurities out, then hammers you into a weapon of divinity in His glory.

As early as preschool, I had this deep understanding that success isn't immediate. All that's ever needed is more reps to refine a skill.

I remember spending weeks taking shot after shot with a regulation-size basketball, trying to sink it into a regulation-height hoop. A hefty task for a four year old.

Weeks went by until the day I made it, then it just clicked. It wasn't long until my parents got me into organized basketball.

But I was having a hard time understanding that it was against the rules to outright tackle kids for the ball.

*That is my fucking ball!*

That instinctual drive—the one that grabs, fights, and claims—has never left me.

Long story short with the basketball: the coach told my parents to put me in football—he was right.

## Empathy vs Anger

Growing up with a father in the Army, I apparently developed quite the dirty mouth—also at an early age.

I carried a vivid memory for years: sitting at the dinner table in Oklahoma when I was around five. My mom came home from work.

The next thing I know, she stormed into the kitchen, clamped her hand around my wrist, and yanked me straight out of my seat. And dragged me to the bathroom.

Without a word, she shoved a ginormous bar of soap in my mouth. Pushes it around while squeezing my jaw with the other hand. She may have said something but I was both terrified and confused—so I couldn't say otherwise.

I learned in a therapy session years later that I told another kid during recess to, "suck my dick."

Ope!

Some memories hide from you—sometimes forever—but they still matter. Even when I didn't know the full story, my soul was already moving toward the light.

Forward motion.

Oh. And for context—I'm an only child...

So, yes, I can absolutely act like a brat sometimes.

"Does not always play well with others," one of my teachers once told my parents. It's true. I can be selfish—though rarely, if at all, it isn't intentionally malicious.

I'm also deeply empathic.

Usually, I can feel something from you before you know what you're feeling, maybe even before you know that you're feeling anything.

Unfortunately, anger started growing right along with my empathy.

(Or at least I was told I was angry...what is it when one doesn't feel accepted for who you are...even at home? Unbelonging?)

An inner war I would never wish upon anyone: Empathy and Anger, battling day and night like Jacob and the angel.

I'm a lot. Like extra everything. I'm well aware. So I get it.

"You're just...a lot," is one of the first things people say to me upon getting to know me. But like with this tone that says "It's a negative for me."

As if being full of passion, emotion, awareness, fire, creativity, love, grief, justice, power, and presence is something I need to apologize for.

I don't take up too much space. I understand I'm kind of a big dude.

**But I own my space.**
**And—I do what I want.**

I'm not aggressive. I'm assertive.
I'm not full of rage. I'm passionately activated.
I'm not unstable. I'm unfiltered.
I'm not speaking as a victim.
I'm speaking from my truth.
I'm not asking for perfection.
I'm asking for your presence.

For balanced effort.
For energy that doesn't just take, but also returns.

I wasn't born angry. I was born to guard what's sacred.

On the surface I'm like a mix of Simon Peter, Matthew, and John the Baptist.

Deep down, I am a divine child named Jonathan.
Translated into God's language (Hebrew): God's Gift

God chose me as a prophet long before I knew it.

But not a prophet in the sense of the word that I'm here to predict anything—like the end of the world. No...that information isn't even in the Holy Bible, and for good reason.

My prophetic duty is to redirect. To help shepherd His sheep back to His voice. Or rather—bring His voice to the sheep who wandered.

I carry His voice, not His throne. I'm not here to chain you to the Pearly Gates—I'm here to bring you home.

I didn't choose this path. God chose it for me. Like orders for a soldier to go to war.

And it took time for me to fully accept His calling...my oh my did I push back.

But I need to circle back to the story of being a kindergartener—telling a kid to suck it.
The other part I remembered in that same therapy session was the fact I was sticking up for another kid—who was getting bullied.

I've always been protective.

I had to be—I was alone most of the time, so it developed early.

Understand this: I don't go looking for fights, but I've ended many.

In elementary school, I was on Bus Patrol. At school my role shifted to Peer Mediator: Helping others through conflict has always been rewarding (foreshadowing).

I was the friend who was friends with everyone. I didn't cling to any one group. I never felt I belonged in one place—at least socially—for long.

I was closer to some friends than others, but I never had tight-knit friendships. Even with the kids in my neighborhood, I loved them all, but I never really felt like I belonged.

I never had those "inseparable best friends"—like the kids in The Goonies—all different, yet always together, unified, no matter what.

One advantage of being an only child is knowing what it feels like to be truly alone—often.

To feel like I didn't fit.
To feel different.
To feel like you belong.
To want nothing more than to be seen.
To have them see my light—and not look away.

With this—I caught constant shit from a few calculated tormentors.

They knew I had a temper—I just don't take kindly to works of evil—and they knew exactly which buttons to push.

Thanks to the tireless efforts of those select few, I spent my fair share of time in the principal's office—ironically, since I was the peer mediator.

They'd poke and prod when no one was looking—until I fucking snapped and made everyone look. It was always my word against all five of theirs.

Back then, most parents didn't give a shit about bullying. "Boys will be boys," they'd say.

Nothing ever really changed in that regard except for me.

## The Catalyst

In junior high something happened. I don't know if the shift was inside me, throughout the entire Universe, or both.

Maybe—it was the new feelings for the ladies (hormones).

Maybe—it was that purposeful feeling I felt from the peer-mediation, but now a void of that feeling.

Maybe—it was how the schoolwork felt incredibly easy and overwhelmingly boring to me.

Maybe—it was the handful of teachers who knocked me down alongside the same student body from elementary.

I had an 8th-grade English teacher who was...overly strict. I swear she had it out for me. I was—extra—in trouble.

She would call us up one by one to hand in assignments—which I did. For the first few weeks, nothing happened.

Then one day, I walked up, handed her my paper, and—without looking up from her grade book—she took it and dropped it straight into the trash.

It happened again. And again.

Finally, I spoke up. As she dropped another assignment into the bin, I asked, "Why do you keep throwing my homework away without looking at it?"

"Because I can't read it," she said. After a pause: "You only got partial credit on the previous assignments because you turned something in, but I can't tell what it is, so..."

And while my parents focused on punishing the teacher, to their right.

I shamed myself, "You can do better."

I "perfected" my handwriting. I practiced over and over, taking my time.

And when I finally made it legible. That's when the comments rolled in: "You write like a girl." "He must be gay." I could go on...

That's when intrusive suicidal thoughts became a regular part of my day. Like tacos are for Tuesdays. Junior high...suicidal thoughts.

It felt like nothing I did mattered, ever. The pain cut deep.

High school was no different.

I stopped going to math classes in 11th grade because the teacher wouldn't actually look at my homework but just call me a liar from his desk when I told him I was done, not done, or almost done.

The answer never mattered. The truth never mattered.

So. Fuck it. Unofficial dropout.

I knew I was different, but I didn't know why. I was trying too hard to fit in where I thought I wanted to belong.

That was only because I didn't understand who I was yet. Or, more honestly—like most of us—I'd forgotten who I was and had yet to remember.

That period of my life was when I learned—sadly—that no one really cares what you're going through, except Jesus.

I had to learn to rely on Jesus, but that lesson wouldn't land for quite some time. And there were many more lessons to come first.

It got so bad I even turned my back on Jesus and never thought I'd look back.

I was unhappy with how life after high school panned out. I was bitter toward God because of it.

Being discharged from the military before I even got my career started—really put a kink in how I envisioned life. As a kid, starting around eight years old, I only saw myself as a Navy SEAL. (Protector vibes?)

Directionless and reeling from a cheating high school sweetheart, I dove head first into a handle of whiskey.

In the four years following my medical discharge from the Navy, I survived two suicide attempts, experienced multiple seizures, and landed in the hospital with a liver functioning at a mere two percent.

I'll always remember the nurse who came back in after the doctor left, looked me dead in the eyes, and said:

"I have a son your age, and this is the mother bear in me coming out: if you don't stop drinking, you will fucking die before you turn twenty-five."

Fuck was that was a kick in the nuts.

I did take a break from drinking, but I didn't put it down completely for a long time.

But on my thirty-eighth birthday, I had one last glass of whiskey with my steak dinner.

That night, God visited me in a dream to remind me of a little deal we made a few years prior. (As of this writing, I no longer drink alcohol—and I haven't for two years now.)

The next morning, I started writing this book—and it flowed onto the page as if the whole thing was already in my head.

I simply needed the obedience to get it out of my head and, ultimately, into your hands (easier said than done).

But before we go there, I have a surprise for you.

## A View From the Outside

I reached out to some people from my past—childhood friends, ex-girlfriends, former clients, my mother—and asked for their unfiltered truth.

How they saw me.
The potential they saw in me that I didn't (or couldn't) yet see.

A raw, uncut account of me from their experiences and perception.

The one you're about to read opened the tear ducts.

***"I first met Jonathan while looking for a new gym—somewhere I could push myself and be challenged by someone who wouldn't let me coast. My first impression of him was sharp: serious, direct, and willing to ask questions that made me confront the ways I was holding myself back, whether through food choices or losing focus on my goals.***

***Jonathan is skilled—no question—but what makes him***

*stand out is the way discipline and empathy collide in him. He can be laser-focused, moving forward with such intensity that the rest of the world fades into black. Compartmentalization doesn't come easily; whatever holds his attention in the present moment consumes him fully, sometimes at the expense of balance, even relationships. But the flip side is refreshing: when Jonathan is with you, he is with you—present in a way that makes the rest of the world disappear.*

*There's also something about him that makes people feel safe. Strangers and friends alike tend to open up, telling him their problems or secrets without hesitation, like he's a built-in sounding board. He listens in a way that feels steady and nonjudgmental—like you can exhale and finally say the thing out loud.*

*He's spontaneous enough to say "let's go" and mean it—whether that's hopping on a plane or diving headfirst into a new pursuit. He's endlessly curious, drawn to big questions and grounded by simple, physical truths like feeling the earth beneath his feet.*

*And for all his intensity, he has his softer edges. Empathy threads through his conversations. Passion sparks in unexpected places. And yes, even discipline yields to indulgence when cheesecake is on the table.*

*Jonathan is a contradiction I've come to admire: serious yet playful, restless yet rooted, unafraid to live with both focus and abandon."*

I really appreciate her and her willingness to do this.

She doesn't know how many tears her little excerpt brought to the surface...happy tears.

I'm grateful for our friendship and what experiences we shared together. And I'm proud of her and the growth I've seen since!

Go after it Megz!

## A Walking Contradiction

I am, in fact, a walking contradiction on most days.

It isn't hypocrisy.
It's a battle I fight every day—the battle no one else sees.

While writing this, I've come to learn that my resistance to God's calling was the catalyst for that looping contradiction.

I was constantly moving from one thing to another, never really satisfied, doubting the whispers from my soul. If I were to write out a resume that contained every job I ever "held;" it would be more pages than this prologue.

Nothing ever seemed to really fit. Even the fitness industry.

But isn't life one big contradiction anyway?

The majority of people spend the majority of their time with their nose to the grindstone—mostly for money—then lack the quality of life once they have time to enjoy the money.

A lot of people are chasing happiness in all the wrong places. Then bitch and moan when it doesn't last or feel as fulfilling as you hoped it would.

We crave peace but continue to feed chaos.

So how can we call life anything other than a contradiction? And yet—how can we say it is only a contradiction?

How do we make any sense of it? Life...I mean—that can't be it—make as much money as possible. By any means possible—and then just—die.

Why does Billy scrub toilets for pennies on the dollar while Brian is CEO of "FlickADick.com" making millions?

(I wouldn't Google that...I literally just made it up but I don't want that in my search history.)

Here's what I know: Contradiction can be a compass.

I can be tender and terrifying.

I can have a Bible in one hand and a barbell in the other.

I can pray with tears flowing with gratitude and drop f-bombs in the same breath.

I can love fiercely and still walk away if it means I keep my self-respect.

The "both/and" isn't a weakness. It's honesty.

Most of the whiplash I've experienced in life was the result of me following *my will* rather than God's.

When I avoided it.
I was split in two.

Purpose vs Performance.

Calling vs Coping.

Passion vs Paycheck.

It felt like my soul was clawing at the very shell other people asked me to wear...and I sadly agreed to do so.

When I surrendered though. When I finally stopped the act.

The tension, stress, and challenges didn't vanish—but I had a clarity that integrated into my faith.

The fire that once scorched my soul was now refining me.

It hurt. It still fucking hurts.

So—if you're a contradiction too, welcome.

Maybe you're not broken—you're just becoming.
And maybe the parts of you that argue aren't enemies; they're instruments waiting to be tuned to the same key.

# Quick Start Guide

If you read the Prologue, you got my backstory. If you skipped it, you didn't miss out on the instructions...

This book isn't a trophy case of my successes.
This book is your map and your compass.

But also—it's a workshop.

You will get dusty.
You will drag old junk out of hidden rooms.
You will probably argue with me—and with God.

Good—
Argue with us.
Toil with yourself and the blueprint laid out in front of you.

If you're willing to let Him tear down what's fake, if you're willing to risk an honest "fuck it" that really means "God, I'm done pretending—do whatever it takes," then you're exactly who this book was written for.

Let's get to work.

**Let's renovate your soul.**

Much of life is shaped—influenced, impacted, traumatized, afflicted, or whatever the fuck else it can be labeled—by other people.

From the bottom rung to the top, other people's choices do hit us. And those hits can sometimes knock us on the ground.

You can't do much about those. Those aren't in your control. Feel them and stand the fuck back up.

That's what you can do.

But then there are our own choices—the only ones we can actually master. The ones we have after we stand back up.

Jesus tells us to offer the other cheek. That's not to say if someone literally knocks you down, you get up and show the the opposite side of your face.

No. "Offering the other cheek" was a fun way to say, offer immediate forgiveness.

In other words, don't seek revenge.

That's the turn: from blame to stewardship.

From victim to agency.

Someone said something close to the effect of: Villains and superheroes both come from the same place—pain. It was what they decided to do with it that made the difference.

A superhero protects people from painful experiences.
A villain afflicts the same pain they experienced to others.

So many fucking choices.

So many variables.

So much impact.

However you make your choices, they matter.

And opening this book might be the most important choice you've made in this moment.

It may or may not be an immediate turning point of your life. I'm not here to fill you with bullshit promises and guarantees. This book isn't about hacks or twelve steps to everything you want in life.

It's not a self-help manual that'll have you drinking warm lemon water at sunrise, cutting carbs for months, buying more rental properties, or selling all your belongings to live in a van.

It's the **raw, unfiltered truth**—anchored in the living word of God, backed by science and logic—and maybe some wit and comedy. That's why this book exists.

It's a mirror.

It's a hammer.

It's a map and a compass.

The thing is—you still have to row your own fucking boat. And I say that with love.

Everything in this book comes from a place of love.

Some chapters might heal you.

Others might piss you the right the fuck off.

All of them are designed to renovate your soul from the inside out. I'll put it kindly, I'm not here to be nice. Nice never got anyone anywhere. But kindness. Love.

Unmeasurable amounts of growth are the fruit of true love and kindness.

This book won't do the work for you. Don't rush it. Don't read it once and shelve it. (Or do, it's your choice...fucking burn it...I wipe the dust from my feet.)

Wrestle with it.
Argue with it.

Write in the margins...plenty of purposefully placed blank pages

Highlight it.

Debate me.
Enlighten me.
I love to learn...but I might debate back...just sayin.

Read it out loud when the silence gets too heavy.

Let it wreck you if need be—then let it help you rebuild yourself—stronger, freer, and closer to God than you've ever been.

Whatever floats your boat.
This is the way back to you.

As you read this—you maybe have those feelings of being lost—and that's okay. Maybe a chapter doesn't resonate—maybe it will later.

Maybe you're already an expert at one particular chapter.
Good—focus on a weakness. Find that chapter.

You can always go back—skip around—or it'll click when God wants it to.

You can even use the chapters as needed.
It really doesn't matter how you use this to renavigate life.
What matters is you use it.

Read it.
Feel it.
Live it.

And if it hits too close to home and the walls start closing in—press pause. Chew on what you read and what it brought to the surface.

Write about it.
Talk about it.

Have a therapist?
Talk it out.

Email me if you need to—or want to.

If you're ready to strip away the bullshit, face His Truth, and start rebuilding from the rubble—take a nice deep breath—grab a sledgehammer, safety goggles, maybe a hardhat, and turn the page.

Because to start; we first have to break down walls you built by the curses of other people's opinions.

# Chapter 1

# Fvck What They Think

**Ego Alert:** You're not "considering feedback." You're renting your life to strangers.

**Vow:** I'm done auditioning. I choose alignment—even if they boo.

# Is This Normal?

Why the actual fuck do we care so much about what other people think? Somewhere along the line, their opinions started weighing more than your own.

The fucked-up part?

Most of the time those "opinions" don't even exist. We imagine them. We conjure them up and build entire storylines in our heads about what someone might say. Then hand the steering wheel of our lives to invisible backseat drivers:

"She wouldn't like that."
"My boss hates me, I'll never get a promotion."
"What will the neighbors think if I build this shed?

The price tag—for caring this much about imaginary thoughts?

**Time** you never get back.
**Creativity** you never ship.
**Peace** you keep mortgaging off to strangers.
**Energy** sucked from your soul.

Simply put, people's opinions are **data, not direction.**

For the fuck sake of Pete, stop.
Stop wasting **your** precious time and energy managing ghosts and their chatter.

This isn't a new problem.

People have been performing for crowds since crowds existed. Our nervous system still believes exile is equivalent to death.

Today, your brain scans for disapproval the way it used to scan for wolves. It's not weakness; it's hardwiring. The work here is learning to hear the alarm without handing it the keys.

**There's a way to handle this:**
Name the courtroom in your head. Who's on the jury? Whose voice is the judge?

Now dismiss the case. New trial. New judge. Your soul.

Seriously—who is "they?" Say their names in your head. Is it a boss? That one aunt? The friend who only claps if you stay small?

Figure out who's noisy in the crowd, because **vague shame is strong and specific shame is weak.**

Then ask the questions that sobers everything up:

*Do they pay my bills, carry my cross, or raise my kids?*
*If not, why are they sitting in the front row of my decisions like they have VIP passes?*

Approval is a drug with no nutrition. It tastes good, hits fast, but you're starving for the next hit by breakfast.

Obedience is slower.
It's quiet. And less sexy.
But fucking builds spine.

So when you feel that "oh no, what will they think" feeling spike—don't fight it.
Don't worship it. Just label it: **"Imagination Jury."**

And then keep walking like you already know the verdict:

**Not guilty. Called. Sent.**

Let me show an example with a story—

## The Man, the Boy, and the Donkey

This is an Aesop fable, a tale older than TikTok, older than Yelp reviews, but still sharp as ever.

A man and his young son were walking to the market with their donkey. The donkey plodded along, hooves tapping the dirt road, while the man and boy walked beside him.

Soon they passed a group of villagers. One scoffed and judged, "Look at those fools. Walking when they've got a donkey to ride!"

So the man lifted his boy onto the donkey's back, and they continued on.

Not far down the road, another crowd jeered. "Lazy brat!" one woman cried. "Making his poor old father walk while he rides in comfort!"

So the man pulled the boy down and climbed onto the donkey himself. The boy trudged beside him, kicking stones.

A few miles later, a farmer shook his head saying, "Shame on you, old man. Making that poor child walk while you sit up there like a king."

Embarrassed, the man pulled his boy back onto the donkey so they both rode. Then, as they reached the town, people began to shout, "Cruelty! Look at those two brutes overloading that poor animal!"

Now the man is in a panic. Every group they passed by found fault.

Desperate to silence the criticism, he and his boy tied the donkey's legs to a pole and hoisted it on their shoulders, carrying it awkwardly through the crowd.

The donkey brayed, kicked, and wriggled until finally it broke free of the ropes, tumbled off the bridge they were crossing, and drowned in the river below.

Trying to please everyone, the man and boy ended up pleasing no one, and losing the very thing they had.

***"For do I now persuade men, or God? Or do I seek to please men? For if I yet pleased men, I should not be the servant of Christ."***
(Galatians 1:10, KJV)

**Translation:** If you live for the comments, you'll die by the edits. That donkey is your life. Keep trying to please everyone else, and you lose it while becoming displeased with yourself.

## Death By Exclusion

This obsession isn't new. It's ancient—wired into our brains back when belonging to a tribe meant life or death. If you were cast out, you weren't just unpopular, you were fucked.

No tribe meant no food. No fire. No protection. Dead.

That survival mechanism is still in our DNA. It's why the thought of being excluded makes our stomachs drop.

But today?

Nobody starves because they didn't get invited to brunch. Yet the brain reacts as if it is definitely going to fucking starve.

Anything in the ballpark of rejection hijacks us, and suddenly imaginary opinions feel real and threatening.

This is happening whether you're aware of it or not.

Psychologists call this the **"spotlight effect"**—the belief that everyone is watching and judging us far more than they really are (Gilovich, Medvec, & Savitsky, 2000).

It gets worse...

Social comparison theory shows we're wired to measure ourselves against others (Festinger, 1954).

Scrolling for ten minutes and your brain has compared your body, bank account, vacation photos—even your damn dog—to mere strangers.

That comparison doesn't just annoy you; it fuels anxiety, depression, and is a prime catalyst for social paralysis.

What's the old saying? "Comparison is the..."

The Holy Bible puts it bluntly:

***"The fear of man bringeth a snare: but whoso putteth his trust in the LORD shall be safe."***
(Proverbs 29:25, KJV)

Fear of people's thoughts is a trap—and we're the idiots who keep walking into it. The only way out—radical self-boundaries.

**Set the Standard:**

**Delete social media:** Get rid of it all. Just the apps. Just for a bit. A modern day fast. It doesn't have to start as something that's permanent.
Have a trusted loved one change your password with a time lock. If later on, you want to make it permanent—that's cool tool.

**Or set rules:** When I open Instagram, I get two scrolls. If nothing hits, I'm out. Not only that, you can work your algorithms to your advantage. What are you consuming?

**Audit your time:** When people tell me they don't have time, their screen time usually tells a different story.

(Unless you're like me and rarely turn the screen off, nor shuts off automatically; resulting in screen-time usage data that looks like I literally do nothing else with my life.)

## The Emperor's New Cloth

This fable is from Hans Christian Andersen.

There once was an emperor obsessed with his appearance. His wardrobe was endless: silks, velvets, gold embroidery.

But vanity never rests.

One day, two swindlers arrived in town claiming they could weave the most magnificent fabric in the world.

It had one magical quality: it was invisible to anyone stupid or unfit for their job.

The emperor, thrilled, paid them handsomely. The swindlers set up looms and pretended to weave.

Ministers came to check progress. Of course, they saw nothing, but terrified of being thought unworthy, they praised the "splendid fabric."

Word spread. Soon the emperor would reveal his new magical clothes.

The day came and the swindlers dressed him in the "robes." Naked, the emperor marched through the streets. And the people, just as afraid of looking stupid, cheered and admired what wasn't there.

Until a child, too innocent to fear judgment, cried out, *"But he isn't wearing anything at all!"*

The truth shattered the illusion.

The emperor blushed, but he marched on, more exposed than ever.

That's what happens when you live off the opinions of other people. You strut around in imaginary clothes, terrified of being seen, until some small voice shouts out the obvious fucking truth. Jesus said,

***"And ye shall know the truth, and the truth shall make you free."*** (John 8:32, KJV)

**2025 translation:** If your worth depends on applause, you'll always be naked. Choose truth over optics.

## When I Listened to Them

**Confession:** I didn't learn that lesson from a book. I learned it the hard way.

When I was seventeen, I didn't want to look like a spineless bitch in front of my friends. With their encouragement, I lit a road flare and shoved it into the urinal of a porta-potty.

Even as I did it, my gut screamed: "Bad idea! You just fucked up!"

But I ignored it. Why?

Because I believed *their* approval mattered more. The fallout was brutal.

A detective showed up. Then court and restitution along with a few thousand hours of community service.

I almost torched my future because I cared more about looking cool than trusting my gut.

That's what happens when you live for "them." They don't even know the weight they carry in your head, yet they're influencing your choices.

This verse from The Gospel of John hits:

***"For they loved the praise of men more than the praise of God."*** (John 12:43, KJV)

My gut was God's mercy, and I ignored it because their approval felt like oxygen.

And I know I'm not the only one in this world who is guilty of this.

## The High Cost of Consensus

Look around.

Everywhere, people are asking: "What do you think about this?"

Yelp reviews.
Facebook recommendations.
TikTok health tips from people with zero qualifications.

The obsession with consensus is toxic.

It looks to me like most people are afraid to pull the trigger on a choice unless they know someone who knows someone's sister who made the exact same choice and got the outcome they're seeking.

**Restaurants:** Some folks won't touch a place with fewer than four stars. Why? Go find out for yourself. I've had incredible meals in one- and two-star joints and garbage food (and service) in five-star spots. Someone else's bad day or picky taste buds shouldn't decide your experiences—or your lack of one.

**HOAs:** Some people landscape their front yard not because they love flowers, but because they're afraid the HOA will send a passive-aggressive letter. For fuck's sake—you're trimming bushes to please people who won't carry your casket.

Here's the truth Scripture reminds us of:

***"The LORD is my light and my salvation; whom shall I fear? the LORD is the strength of my life; of whom shall I be afraid?"*** (Psalm 27:1, KJV)

**Translation:** The only opinion that ultimately matters doesn't come from Yelp, Instagram, or Karen from the HOA. It comes from above. And for my secular friends—it comes from the space between your ears, which is ironically still...from above the rest of you.

**However:** I ask we all obey safety and legal requirements; just don't outsource your soul—or your front porch—to a committee.

**Influencer Culture:** A 22-year-old sipping a latte in Bali telling you how to "manifest abundance;" is not a way to learn how to "manifest abundance."

Meanwhile, you're in line at Walmart, wondering if getting the generic cereal means you're lacking abundance (rather than the reality of being disciplined with a budget).

**Spoiler:** no one in Bali is paying your fucking bills.

**The Influencer Audit:** Before you take advice directly or indirectly, ask yourself these questions.

1. Are they qualified—or just charismatic?

2. Are they accountable to anyone but their following?

3. Do they profit if I believe them?

If the answers smell like optics, it's a hard pass.

Choose truth over applause.

## Everest and the Neighbors

Close the app.
Step off the HOA porch.

Look up.

There's a mountain with your name on it—no committee, no algorithm, no "Karen" will climb it for you. This is where approval ends and courage begins.

Think of Everest. People die trying to climb it.

Does that stop others? Nope.

- Some see the risk and say, "Not worth it."
- Others say, "Absolutely fucking worth it."

Look at Nims Purja. Everest wasn't enough for one season for that guy. He completed all *fourteen* summits over 8,000 meters in six months and a few days. He did what the last person took ***years*** to accomplish.

Everyone has a metaphorical Everest—or set of peaks to summit.
Something massive they want to conquer. To pave a path.

What's yours?
What's the thing you'd regret never attempting?

And who's talking you out of it—*them*, or *you*?

**Warning:** Most of the people you're worried about, or listening to, wouldn't even attempt their own Everest.

Don't let them convince you not to climb yours.

Impostor syndrome creeps in here, too.

Psychologists Clance and Imes (1978) found that even high achievers often believe they're frauds—terrified of being "found out." That's the ego talking, fed by the imaginary opinions of "*them.*"

God reminded Joshua when he faced his own Everest:

***"Have not I commanded thee? Be strong and of a good courage; be not afraid, neither be thou dismayed: for the LORD thy God is with thee whithersoever thou goest."*** (Joshua 1:9, KJV)

That same courage is available to you—if you stop handing the steering wheel to people who won't even back out of their own driveway.

## Peer Pressure Gets a Blazer

Courage isn't just for mountains; it's also for rooms where everyone's nodding along to what you know is wrong.

Peer pressure doesn't disappear after high school—it grows up, buys a blazer, and calls itself "best practice."

In a classic psychology study, researchers showed participants two lines and had actors intentionally give the wrong answer to which line was visually longer.

The lines were obviously different lengths and the real participant—the only one not in on it—argued at first.However, would eventually cave and agree with the group of actor participants.(Asch, 1951).

They literally betrayed their own perception of what they knew was true just to avoid standing out in opposition of the crowd.

That's the power of social pressure.

Your body reads rejection as danger; your heart rate increases, your gut becomes a rope artist, and your brain begs you to blend in.

This is why fashion trends take off: some influencer wears a pair of jeans that look like they were washed in a garbage disposal. Suddenly everyone's lining up to pay $200 for purposely ripped denim.

It's not style; it's conformity.

You bite your tongue in meetings, agree with bullshit opinions, or stay silent when your gut screams otherwise.

Why? To be liked? To avoid conflict?

To "feel" safe.

I've been there. Maybe you have, too. You don't have to stay in that place. I didn't. You *do* have the same choice I have.

I get it's not easy to admit the choice is in front of you, but it is.

Scripture doesn't let us off the hook either:

***"And be not conformed to this world: but be ye transformed by the renewing of your mind, that ye may prove what is that good, and acceptable, and perfect, will of God."*** (Romans 12:2, KJV)

Following the crowd may feel safe, but it's also a slow rot to your soul. Subtle. Sometimes even unnoticeable.

And transformation only happens when you step out of the line.

Get out of that fucking line.

You don't have to blow up the room—please don't—but you don't have to betray your mind, your gut, or your soul.

## Guard Your Fucks & Build Your Table

Plot twist! It's not about not giving a fuck at all. It's about choosing carefully where you spend what fucks you have to give.

Your "give-a-fuck bucket" is small.

Protect it. Address any leaks promptly and thoroughly.

*(Gratitude note: Credit to* ***Mark Manson*** *and his book* ***"The Subtle Art of Not Giving a Fck*."*** *It planted the seed for choosing where to care. If this chapter hits, that book helped sharpen this particular blade.)*

Some people *do* deserve your fucks: mentors, therapists, coaches, loved ones (sometimes)—the people who challenge you with uncomfortable truths because they actually fucking care about you growing into your potential.

Maybe even more so than you do for yourself.

Something I always told clients was:

"One of my jobs in serving you is to believe in you until you learn to believe in yourself."

I've been that person for others many many times in life.

It's both exhilarating to watch someone's growth and difficult to be the person to deliver those hard-truth moments that growth requires.

Jim Rohn said, *"You are the average of the five people you spend the most time with."*

Choose your fucking people wisely.

And if you need a little more Scripture to back it up:

***"He that walketh with wise men shall be wise: but a companion of fools shall be destroyed."***
(Proverbs 13:20, KJV)

**Translation:** Be picky with who sits at ***your*** table. And be just as selective when someone is inviting you to sit at their table.

This is the work—the inner work—the messy, uncomfortable process of asking:

**"Who am I? Who am I without the masks, the filters, the performance?"**

Because when you don't, you can get stuck in the dark.

And in that dark, your best tools—intuition, compassion, energy for life, your inner child—start to shut down.

The right people around you?

They're your **candles**.
They are the light for your darkness.

# Find Your Candles

Ignore your gut long enough, keep it in the dark long enough, it will go silent.

Your cage, the one you feel stuck in, was built from "them," from what you think they think, from the influences leading you *away* from your purpose.

Including any voices only you can hear—and no, you're not crazy—but only you can silence them.

Jesus put it this way:

***"But seek ye first the kingdom of God, and his righteousness; and all these things shall be added unto you."*** (Matthew 6:33, KJV)

Put God's voice first—the rest will take care of itself.

And for my secular friends—put yourself first...even you mothers out there.

The better you take care of yourself—the better you can serve your beloved.

**Try this:**

Name three candles by name.
Text or call one.
Pray or sit in silence with God/Universe for one minute.

Then ask: *Which voice gets my next yes?*

## The Paradox

This is where it gets deliciously twisted.

Say it with me: "I don't give a fuck what you think of me."

Good—how did that feel?

In the same respect, I don't give a fuck if you like this book.

I'm not here to be nice.
I'm not here to appease or validate what you already believe.
I care about **serving** you.

I'm not here to reinvent your wheel—I'm here to help you remember how your wheel works and why it doesn't need reinventing.

I spend my limited "give-a-fuck bucket" on certain truths, my craft, my calling, and my five (God, my candles, and a select few VIPs who have earned a vote).

**Approval is optional. Alignment is mandatory.**

**Practical checkpoint:**

Before you take my words (or anyone's), ask:

Does this help me become, or just help me belong?

If no one ever knew I did it, would I still do it?

Is this aligned with God's voice—or with "theirs"?

Keep the paradox.
Lose the permission slip.

We're here to move.

## The Application Gap

The self-help industry is worth billions—books, seminars, podcasts.

But most people don't apply a damn thing.
Most I see—they read for conversation, not transformation.

Knowledge without application is just trivia—and most of this won't even help you win trivia night at the local pub.

The difference between stuck and free isn't what you know; it's what you do with what you know.

I'm not handing you hacks or shortcuts.
I'm asking you to do the uncomfortable—unsexy work you don't

see going viral on TikTok: choose whose voices matter and ***silence*** the rest.

Even if that means excusing people from your table.

Even if it hurts.
Even if it feels lonely at first.

If you need to hire your table—therapists, coaches, mentors—do it.

But please; make sure they live by what they preach.

Check their receipts: fruit, boundaries, integrity, accountability. They need to be authentic, real, and unfiltered.

As the saying goes, "Never go to a dentist with wooden teeth."

**Action: Close the Gap**

1. Write down **five** names—who gets a vote in your life.

2. Choose **one** hard conversation or boundary you've been avoiding.

3. Book it. Put it on the calendar. *If it's not scheduled, it's not real.*

Consumption is easy.
Application is freedom.

# The Sower

Jesus tells a story about a farmer throwing seed.

Same seed—four outcomes—because the difference isn't the seed...it's where the seed lands.

And He flat-out explains it:

***"The seed is the word of God"*** (Luke 8:11, KJV)

So the question isn't "Is God speaking?"
The question is: **What kind of soil is my life right now?**

Same truth, same warning—just in our language:

Your life, your calling, your faith, your morals and values, literally everything else—it's a seed. And the "cares of the world"—*What will they think? How many likes did I get?*—will choke you and leave you fruitless.

It all depends on where you throw the seed.

**Soil types in today's language:**

**Path**: drive-by opinions, cynics, the crowd. Leave your seed on the sidewalk and the scavengers will eat it.

**Rocky ground:** hype without roots—motivation spikes, then dies. No practices, no depth, no system, no discipline, no staying power.

**Thorns:** metrics and money as masters—approval, optics, "success" that strangles the root system.

**Good soil:** quiet obedience, chosen voices (your five), daily disciplines (prayer, training, service), boundaries (the two-scroll rule).

**Quick soil audit:**
Where is your seed right now—path, rock, thorns, or good soil

What's one thorn to cut today (a feed, a room, a voice)?

What's one root to plant (Scripture, prayer, a call to a candle, a rep in the gym)?

Plant in good soil. Guard it. Water it.
The crop comes later—always later—but it comes.

## Field Work: Dismiss the Jury

**Purpose:** Stop living like you're on trial in a courtroom that isn't even real.

**Time:** 15 minutes

**Tools:** Pen + paper (or Notes app) + your calendar.

### Step 1 — Name the Courtroom
Write this at the top of the page: **THE COURT OF:**

(Example: *The Court of "Don't Embarrass Yourself,"* or *The Court of "Be Liked."*)

Now list the **jury**—the people whose opinions you keep imagining. Include the ridiculous ones.

Yes, even the "random dude from high school" and "Karen from the HOA." Don't hold back and be honest for the love of fuck.

Write them all down.

Every source of mouth-breathing blasphemy.

## Step 2 — Choose Your Five

Your give-a-fuck bucket is small and you pick who gets a vote.

Write **five names** at the top of a new list: These are your **candles**—the voices that actually bring light, not noise.

(And yes—God can be one of the five. In fact...He is the brightest candle available to anyone.)

## Step 3 — Kick Everyone Else Out

Go back to the jury list and write one sentence next to each name: **"No vote."**

Not "I hate you."
Not "You're wrong."
Just: **No vote.**

### Step 4 — The Soil Cut

Quick audit: where is your seed being tossed right now—**path, rock, thorns, or good soil?**

Now do one of each:

**One thorn to cut today:** A feed. A room. A person. A habit. A scroll.
**One root to plant today:** Prayer. Scripture. A gym sesh. A call/text to a candle.

### Step 5 — Book It

Pick **one hard conversation or boundary** you've been avoiding. Then schedule it.

If it's not on the calendar, it's not real.

**Receipts:**
Screenshot the calendar event **or** send a text to one candle: **"I'm practicing 'fuck what they think.' Ask me tonight if I kept my boundary."**

**One-line reflection:**
Before you say yes to anything this week, ask: **"Does this help me become…or just help me belong?"**

## Wrapping Up

At the end of the day, it's your ego that cares so deeply about what others think.

The real you—the truest, brightest, most alive version of you—doesn't give a single fuck.

Because that version of you knows freedom isn't found in applause; it's found in obedience—to your calling, to your Creator, to that quiet pull in your gut that's been whispering "this isn't you."

And that whisper started the day you started believing "them."

The ego is a little PR manager with a clipboard—obsessed with optics, terrified of rejection, addicted to being approved.

It will sell you a smaller life and call it "being realistic."

Every time you silence your truth to please "them," ***you*** weld another bar onto your own fucking cage.

But every time you choose your authenticity self over their approval, you pry those bars open a little wider. And yeah, it might be loud as you pry. Good—let it be known. That's the sound of freedom.

This is not rebellion for rebellion's sake—but this is sacred rebellion.

The kind that says, *"I'd rather disappoint the world than betray my soul."*
The kind that stops asking for permission from people who aren't living your life.
The kind that no longer allows another person to influence what "you should" be doing with your life.

# FVCK IT

**Psychology** calls it individuation—becoming the fullest expression of who you are meant to be.
**Faith** calls it surrender—laying down the mask so your spirit can breathe.

Either way, it's the same doorway.

You're the one who has to walk through.
Let the weight of "what they think" slide off your shoulders like an old coat that never fit right.

You've outgrown it.
You've outgrown their opinions, their timelines, their tiny little fucking expectations—which have more to do with controlling you than anything else.

The only opinion that ever mattered—God's—already called you enough.

And when you finally meet that version of yourself—the one who laughs louder, moves freer, trusts deeper—you'll recognize a little extra sparkle in your eyes.

Because you're no longer powered by ego.
You're plugged into the power of the Spirit.

And the sooner you meet you, the sooner your life truly begins—not the life you were told to live—the one you're meant to love living.

You start living the life you were born to build.
So fuck what they think.

Go on now git—Meet yourself.

And congratulations—you've learned it's okay to kick "them" out of the driver's seat.
Now—let's check if anyone else still has a hand on the wheel.

# Chapter 2
# Fvck Up
# Your
# Ego

**Ego Alert:** Your ego doesn't need healing—it needs the backseat, with a rear-facing child carrier, and a five-point harness.

**Vow:** My ego can scream from the back but when God says go—I go.

## Meet Your Loudest Enemy

The crowd is quiet now.
The neighbors, Karen, the HOA, the keyboard warriors—still chirping—but the volume is at least low enough you can't make out what they're saying.

Do you hear the peace in the silence?
Or do you still hear that—one other voice?

It's fucking weird too—because it sounds like your own voice.

The one constantly rehearsing your fears, bargaining with your worth, and narrating worst-case scenarios like some kind of prophetic fortune cookie.

"Keep your friends close and your enemies closer," they say.

I call bullshit.

Because your greatest enemy already lives in your head.Twenty-four-fucking-seven.
Whether you like it or not.
Completely rent free.

I'd even argue it is the ***only*** true enemy in your life.

**Your Ego.**

Your Ego is a shitty student film producer with poor editing skills and a cast of one *trying* too fucking hard to impress the

class.
Or that drunk uncle at Thanksgiving.

He thinks he's the smartest guy in the room, he's definitely the loudest, he won't shut up, he dominates nearly every conversation.

Worst of all—he actually believes his own bullshit.

The problem isn't the uncle.
The problem is you keep sitting next to him and listening.

**Your soul needs a bouncer, not a bartender.**

The one-two punch:
1) Your ego is **not** you.
2) If you don't put it in its place, it will drive your life into a ditch full of misery.

Neuroscience calls it an occurrence in the brain dubbed—the **Default Mode Network** (DMN)—the self-referential channel that loops old stories, comparisons, and worst-case scenarios.

Psychology calls it **Ego**.
The Holy Bible calls it **Pride**.

Whatever you name it, it's the same damn thing:
a voice loud enough to drown out your Spirit. And until you recognize it, it runs the show.

The thing is—your Ego doesn't want to protect you; its mission is **preservation**.

To preserve the lie you've built your entire life around.

**It is *the* curator of your biggest, oldest, pile of bullshit.**

The Ego's favorite trick is sounding like God, or yourself, but even the Devil quoted scripture to Jesus—and your *Soul* needs a filter of some kind.

Here is your **15-second Spiritual Fire-Alarm**:
You cannot un-invite the drunk uncle from your head, but you can learn to interrupt him. This is a fast, three-step firewall to get your soul back in the driver's seat.

**Name it:** *"That's ego."* (It's a role, not your identity.)

**Acknowledge it:** *"Thanks for trying to keep me safe."* (Compassion cuts the intensity of the charge.)

**Redirect it:** *"I've got it—we're choosing obedience over optics."* (Choose God's will—or your own—over the crowd's applause and criticism.)

Your Ego is not your friend.
Your Ego is a squatter dressed in your favorite clothes.

There's no demolition crew for this one.
And the eviction notice didn't do a damn thing.

But at least now, you're talking to your Ego rather than **allowing** it to speak for you.

# The Frog and the Ox

This is your Ego's playbook in the form of a fable...

One day, a frog hopped into a meadow where an ox was grazing.

The frog watched in awe.

This ox was huge, powerful, and majestic.

The frog, small and jealous, croaked, "I want to be as big as that ox!"

So he puffed himself up.
His sides stretched.
His cheeks bulged.

"Am I as big as the ox yet?" he asked his friends.
They shook their heads. "Not even close."

The frog inhaled more. "Now?" he wheezed.
"Still smaller," they croaked back.

Determined, the frog took one final, massive gulp of air. His body stretched to its breaking point.

And with a loud pop, he exploded.

That's ego.

Always puffing itself up.
Always comparing.
Always chasing more until it bursts.

This is especially true with the fatal act of comparison.
It's an obsession the Ego has that can push you until you pop.

Life is not about becoming the Ox.

It's about becoming the best Frog you can fucking become.
You don't need a bigger you.

You need a truer you.

And that starts by recognizing the Ego for what it is: desperate, insecure, and self-appointed manager of your soul.

It's a spiritual steroid that may make you appear big but leaves your soul brittle.

***"Pride goeth before destruction, and an haughty spirit before a fall."*** (Proverbs 16:18, KJV)

This verse isn't a warning.
It's a fucking roadmap.

And demoting your Ego from the driver seat to a passenger in the back—well that's just the first battle.

# Spiritual Ego

The Ego is in the backseat now—but remember—drunk uncle. So he also has a tendency to be the forever-annoying backseat driver. But this helps us by exposing your Ego's favorite lie:

*"You're in control."*

Pride and Ego go hand in hand—and both pretty much guarantee a face-plant.

They aren't just "bad traits;" they act as survival strategies. And they are disastrous about it.

They'll have you performing for people who don't matter or even respect you—while at the same time ignoring the ones who do.

They keep you looking at a mirror when you need a compass and a map.

The Ego wants to protect its narrative but make it seem like it's protecting you.

*"I'm good. I'm smart. I'm right."*

You're full of stinky ass shit.

But your soul wants the raw fucking truth, no matter how much it hurts.

Your soul knows the truth is the only thing that actually heals.

This is why every spiritual journey is not an ascent.
At least not a true journey—the Ego can be deceitful.

Jesus wasn't the Messiah people expected Him to be.
He didn't wage war on the Romans.
His war was against sin.

Jesus didn't just invite people to follow Him around; he invited them to die:
*Death to their old narratives, their aged reputations, and their pride.*

***"Whosoever will come after me, let him deny himself, and take up his cross, and follow me."***
(Mark 8:34, KJV)

Deny *himself.*
Not deny cheesecake.
Deny the self. Deny the **Ego**—

The thing you hired as your production manager when you became old enough to compare your gorgeous Froggy self to that beautiful, big Ox.

You're a fucking frog. Be a frog.

It's not just the obvious Pride, either—the loud, arrogant, "I'm better than you" kind of Ego.

That's the easy one to spot.

I'm talking about the **Spiritual Ego**: the shadow-self that uses your good intentions as a disguise.

The Spiritual Ego is the one who performs:

## 1) Boundaries:

"I don't need boundaries. I'm not like *those* people."
"I can handle it."
*(Meanwhile your nervous system is begging for a locked door.)*

## 2) People-pleasing dressed up as "love:"

"I just want everyone to be okay."
"If they're disappointed in me, I'm the problem."
"I'll just betray myself first—faster, cleaner."

## 3) Being "unbothered" as emotional avoidance:

"I don't get triggered."
"I don't do drama."
"I just quietly disappear and call it peace."

## 4) Forgiveness used as a shortcut around grief:

"I'm over it."
"I don't need to talk about it."
"If I admit it still hurts...then it it'll be a big deal."

## 5) "High vibration" as control:

"I can't be around negativity. I need to protect my peace."
Translation: "I can't tolerate real human feelings unless they're convenient."

"So I'll curate my life instead of living it."

## 6) Humility used to hide jealousy:

"I'm happy for them."
"I just...don't understand why it's never me."
"So I'll smile while I shrink."

## 7) Service as self-erasure:

"I'm here to help."
"People need me."
"And if I stop being useful, I'm terrified I'll stop being wanted."

## 8) Manifesting as self-blame:

"If I were truly aligned, this wouldn't be happening."
"So this pain must be my fault."
"And somehow that feels safer than admitting life is brutal sometimes."

## 9) "I'm detached" as intimacy-phobia:

"I'm not attached to outcomes."
"I'm not attached to people either."
"Because attachment might mean I actually have something to lose."

## 10) Growth language to excuse staying in a bad situation:

“This is teaching me a lesson.”
“Maybe I’m supposed to endure it.”
“Maybe I’m just scared to admit I’m allowed to leave.”

## 11) Being “the bigger person” as silent self-harm:

“I’ll be the bigger person—I’ll swallow it.”

(Then silently resent everyone for not noticing your sacrifice.)

## 12) Toxic gratitude:

“I should be grateful.”
“Other people have it worse.”
“I’ll call my suffering ‘perspective’ and keep bleeding politely.”

This is nothing more than constant comparison between reality and the manufacturing of what you *think* life should be.

It’s the lie that says, *“Your work is your worth.”*

It’s a **spiritual treadmill** that never stops, never satisfies, and always demands a higher price.

Keep this in mind:
**Humility isn’t humiliation.**

Control tries to script everyone and everything.

And everyone around you can tell.

Surrender control and the actions of others become just input: effort, integrity, obedience.

There's no control.
There's no manipulation.

But you still have choices within your control.

## **Control vs. Surrender**:

Outcome-fixated vs. Faithful Process

Image management vs. Character formation

Protect reputation vs. Tell the truth

Delay to be "ready" vs. Ship, then refine

## **"Release the Wheel" Drill**:

1. Exhale slow. Shoulders down.

2. Name it: "That's ego wanting control."

3. Pray/declare: "God, I release the outcome. Show me the next faithful step."

4. Write one step.

5. Do it now. (If >2 minutes, schedule it. If <2 minutes, move.)

## The Ego's Core Lie: Performance is Protection

When you were a child, you needed a safe place to land—like anyone. When the house was unstable—in any way, shape, or form—you started building a reputation inside yourself.

That reputation became your armor.

Maybe you were the (extra) good kid to keep the peace between your parents.

Maybe you were the overachiever for the compliment.

Maybe you learned to silence your truth because your truth didn't matter—when it mattered most.

**The Ego said:**
**Perform for them, and you'll be safe from them.**

What you don't know is later on—the armor becomes a cage.The performance becomes a prison.

Even if you have people applauding your performance.
It feels like you're on the solitary side of a zoo exhibit.

Everyone's watching and cheering and enjoying your Ego while your truest self feels alone, unseen, and rejected.

That truest form of you—your Soul and your Spirit.

Imprisoned.

Restrained.

Caged up.

Jesus said,

***"Verily I say unto you, Except ye be converted, and become as little children, ye shall not enter into the kingdom of heaven,"*** (Matthew 18:3, KJV)

My homie there is telling you to **drop the fucking armor**.

The World—God—The Universe—doesn't want or need your performance; your presence is what it demands.

The presence of your Soul and Spirit—shining its Light into the world around you is what works best.

That's what really gets people's attention.

Regardless of who you believe pieced you together.
I mean—the real you.

That's **presence**.

**Not** perfection.
**Not** performance.
**Not** pride.

**Presence.**

Presence is the light. And where there is light, there must also be darkness.

## The Shadow: A Closet Door The Ego Won't Open

Carl Jung took it further: we all carry a shadow—the parts of ourselves we desperately hide. Jealousy, anger, selfishness, lust— (Jung, 1959/1968).

The shadow is like a closet so overstuffed you can't even close the door.

And the ego?

It's the frantic homeowner shoving everything back in before company comes over.

Here's the **Spiritual Geometry**—the problem—of your downfall:

The junk doesn't disappear.
The more you hide it, the more power it gains.
Left unattended, it festers, and your anxiety climbs right along with it.

***"And the light shineth in darkness; and the darkness comprehended it not."*** (John 1:5, KJV)

Facing your shadow isn't about shaming yourself for having darkness; it's about **dragging it into the light**, where secrecy loses its grip.

Your ***whole*** self isn't in the light, and that is the real problem to your Soul and Spirit.

## **What the Shadow Looks Like in Real Life**:

**Overreactions:** 2/10 provocation, 10/10 explosive rage.

**Moral Grandstanding:** Preaching hard against what secretly tempts you.

**Numbing Cycles**: Porn, doom scrolling, overwork, that "one drink" becoming seven.

**Spiritual Bypass**: Using Bible verses as band-aids over unacknowledged wounds.

**Perfectionism:** Control disguised as excellence and superiority.

### **What the Ego Does With the Shadow**:

The Ego is the shadow's bodyguard *and* drinking buddy. Its defensive moves are highly predictable:

**Deny:** *That's not me.*

**Minimize:** *It's not that bad.*

**Project:** *It's their fault.*

**Perform:** *If I look good, I am good.*

**Reframe:** Humility ≠ humiliation.

Humility is reality-based ownership: *this lives in me—so I'll name it, tame it, and give it to God.*

## Two-minute light practice:

This is your fast-track surrender. If it takes less than two minutes, do it now...

1. **Name it:** *Jealousy. Rage. Lust. Control.*
2. **Own it:** *This is mine to steward—not to hide.*
3. **Bring it to God:** *Father, shine Your light here. Trade my secrecy for strength.*
4. **One Next Step:** Text a candle (trusted friend/ mentor), book a therapy session, or set a boundary.

Your shadow needs **witnesses, not an audience**.

Telling your candles is not telling the entire internet.

And if it ends up out there, it might be time to blow a candle out.

But most people don't face it. They won't face it.

I get it. It's fucking scary.

So instead, we wear masks.

And these masks don't just isolate you on the inside—they break connections with everyone around you.

## The Bundle of Sticks

There once was a father with a house full of bickering, arrogant sons.

Every damn day they were at each other's throats—arguing, competing, puffing up their egos. Always quick to swing fists over the dumbest shit.

The father grew weary of it. He knew words wouldn't cut through their pride, so he tried something different.

He gathered them in the yard and laid down a bundle of dry sticks, tied tight with cord.

"Break these," he commanded.

Each son stepped forward, each chest puffed a little bigger than the last.
One by one, each son strained, bent, and twisted, but the bundle wouldn't break.

They all failed.

Then the father cut the cord. The sticks scattered across the ground.

"Now," he said, "break them."

In seconds, the boys snapped each stick with a crack and a grin.

Alone, the sticks were nothing.
Together? They were unbreakable.

The father looked at his sons. **"This is you, you arrogant little asses. Alone, each of you is as fragile as straw. Together, you're as tough as iron."**

The Ego isolates.

The Ego says, "I don't need anyone. I can do this alone." But scripture slaps that lie in the face:

***"And if one prevail against him, two shall withstand him; and a threefold cord is not quickly broken."*** (Ecclesiastes 4:12, KJV)

Your ego whispers independence, but freedom often comes from unity.

Through connection.

And connection is hindered when there's a mask.

Drop the mask.

Drop the puffed-up bullshit.

Bind yourself to others who sharpen you, and watch how much harder you are to break.

***"I returned, and saw under the sun, that the race is not to the swift, nor the battle to the strong, neither yet bread to the wise, nor yet riches to men of understanding, nor yet favour to men of skill; but time and chance happeneth to them all"***
(Ecclesiastes 9:11, KJV)

# The Masks We Wear

Your ego is a world-class costume designer.

To protect you from rejection, it hands you masks:

- **The Hero:** always saving everyone else so you never deal with your own shit.

- **The Martyr:** suffering loudly so people see how "good" you are.
- **The Clown:** cracking jokes to hide the pain that's eating you alive.
- **The Chameleon:** changing colors to fit in, terrified of standing out.
- **The Lone Wolf:** pretending you don't need anyone so you can't get hurt.

*There's more, but you know your costume wardrobe better than I do. Do some research.*

Hell, I've worn the Clown and Lone Wolf costumes so often I should have gotten a SAG card by now.

**Here's the truth:** These masks once served you. They protected you when being you felt unsafe. But as an adult? They choke the life out of you.

***"For the good that I would I do not: but the evil which I would not, that I do."*** (Romans 7:19, KJV)

That's the ego running scripts you don't even fully believe anymore.

**Unmask: Spot it → Swap it**

1. **Name the mask**
   (Hero, Martyr, Clown, Chameleon, Lone Wolf).

2. **Name the fear** it's protecting: (rejection, being seen, losing control, abandonment).

3. **Swap the behavior** for one honest move:
   **Hero** → ask, "Who asked?" Then do *your* next step.
   **Martyr** → ask for help once, without the halo.
   **Clown** → say one real sentence: "I'm not okay today."
   **Chameleon** → state one preference out loud.
   **Lone Wolf** → text a candle and tell the truth.

4. **Pray/declare/affirm:** "God, I choose truth over disguise. Spirit drives."

Masks kept you safe then.
Truth frees you now.

We've named the masks—the fears underneath them.
Now let's pop the hood and look at the wiring that keeps us playing dress up on the daily.

## The Science of Ego

I love neuroscience don't you?
It's a wiring schematic for a better understanding of the brain.

Remember the **default mode network (DMN)?**

When you're overthinking, replaying arguments, or comparing yourself to strangers on Instagram, this DMN is the one system lights up (Raichle et al., 2001).

Think of the DMN as the Ego's control room: it spins stories, builds identities, and glues you to the past and the future.

And the sick joke? The DMN is most active when you're "at rest."

So sitting in silence is precisely when your mind starts performing a full Broadway production titled something like:

**"Remember Every Embarrassing Moment Ever"**

No wonder people avoid silence and stillness like it's the plague. Stillness forces you to face the loudest roommate in your head.

(Which if you haven't learned to be okay with that encounter. Work on it—it's more helpful than it is scary.)

There's good news though—leverage: Your brain also has a **task-positive network (TPN)**—the focus system you use when you're present, solving a concrete problem, serving someone, or praying with intention.

DMN and TPN work like a see-saw: when one goes up, the other goes down...at least—generally. There are always margins of error.

Me personally—both of these network systems work simultaneously in my brains.

Yes—I said brains.

Typically though; training the TPN and the DMN eventually quiets down for the most part.

Research broadly shows a few patterns worth using:

**Mindful attention** and **prayerful focus** reduce DMN chatter and rumination over time (e.g., meditation studies reporting decreased DMN activity/connectivity).

**Body engagement** (lifting, walking, even washing dishes with full attention) nudges you into TPN—present, grounded, quieter inside.

**Mind-wandering** correlates with decreased happiness (Killingsworth & Gilbert, 2010).

**Translation:** drifting with the DMN isn't just noisy—it's costly.

You won't silence your Ego by arguing with it; you starve it with rebellious attention.

DMN → TPN: Fast Switches

1. **Name + Notice:**
   *That's DMN.* Say it out loud or in your head. Then list 5 things you can see, 4 you can feel, 3 you can hear, 2 you can smell, 1 you can taste. Senses pull you into TPN—now.

2. **Prayer-Breath:**
   Repeat 6–8 cycles. Longer exhales downshift arousal; short mantra = anchored attention.

   Inhale 4 counts: *"Be with me."*Exhale 6 counts: *"I release control."*

3. **Two-Minute Task:**
   Pick one tiny action aligned with your values.Send the honest text, wash five dishes, write three sentences, do 20 air squats, open the document and title the page.
   Doing flips the DMN/\TPN see-saw.

4. **Single-Point Focus:**
   Stare at one object (a candle, cross, tree). Notice only that thing. When DMN interrupts, label it *"thinking"* and return.

   Fail a hundred times?
   Perfect—every return rep is a rep.

5. **Serve Right Now:**
   Ask, "What's one small way to serve a person in reach?"
   Then do it.
   Service is TPN rocket fuel.

**DMN (Ego):** story teller, past/future, reputation, rumination.

**TPN (Spirit-led focus):** presence, next faithful step, obedience.

We're not trying to kill the narrator.

We're just no longer letting it drive.

## The Empty Boat

A man is rowing his boat up river. Suddenly, he notices another boat coming right toward him.

He yells and screams for it to move.

It doesn't and the boats collide.

The man—he explodes—screaming and cursing damnation. Ready to burn the world to the ground.

Then—he sees it.

The other boat is empty. His rage—evaporates instantly.

That's Ego.

It wants you to take everything personally.
But more than half the time, the "other boat" is empty.

Jesus cut through the thick of it:

***"...Father, forgive them; for they know not what they do."*** (Luke 23:34, KJV)

Ego personalizes everything.
Spirit forgives everything.

## My Empthy Boat Moment

On a freezing cold morning in March 2024, I stepped into my garage. And without warning—I broke.

Shaking. Sobbing.
Sweating like someone doing hot yoga in a confessional booth.

Not because of one bad day.
Because I finally realized I wasn't who I thought I was.

I wasn't my job.
I wasn't my relationships.
I wasn't my bank account.
I wasn't my social media feed.
I wasn't even the voice in my head.

That voice—the one screaming lies and irreversible violent conclusions—was my ego.

Back at it again.
But for the first time, I didn't fight back.

I faced him.
I sat with him.
I listened to him.

Then—I told him,

"I see you. You've tried to protect me and you're still trying to. And I understand why. But I don't want you driving anymore. Please get in the back. Buckle up. And watch how I drive."

For the first time, I felt free. Unchained.

Paul described this battlefield:

***"For the flesh lusteth against the Spirit, and the Spirit against the flesh: and these are contrary the one to the other: so that ye cannot do the things that ye would."*** (Galatians 5:17, KJV)

The floor of my garage became the battlefield—
Ego versus Spirit—the moment I accepted I wasn't living my purpose and how important it was for that to happen.

Even Jesus had smoke for puffed-up egos, maybe then, we should take the hint.

Jesus told a story that hits ego straight in the gut.

## Pharisees, Pride, and Jesus' Roast

Two men went to the temple to pray.

One was a Pharisee—polished, respected, loud about how righteous he was. He stood tall and prayed loudly: *"God, I thank you that I'm not like other men; robbers, evildoers, even like this tax collector. I fast twice a week and give a tenth of all I get."*

Meanwhile the tax collector stood at a distance, wouldn't even lift his eyes up to heaven. He beat his chest and prayed, *"God, have mercy on me, a sinner."*

Jesus said it was the tax collector, not the Pharisee, who went home justified.

Because God sees through ego.

***"I tell you, this man went down to his house justified rather than the other: for every one that exalteth himself shall be abased; and he that humbleth himself shall be exalted."*** (Luke 18:14, KJV)

Parable received.
Pride exposed.

If "My Empty Boat" moment taught you anything, it's this: **most collisions with an empty boat are with our own reflection.**

The Pharisee polishes his mirror.
The tax collector smashes his.

But here's the hard pivot—we must stop fantasizing about ***sinking*** the ship.

## The Ego Death Trip

Some folks chase "ego death" with heroic doses or ten-day sits

I'm guilty of it.
I spent years chasing the death of mine.

And don't get me wrong—those peak moments—can be absolutely beautiful.

Sacred.
Even holy.

But we need a paradigm shift about the reality that is—the ego.
From "kill the ego" to "integrate it."

Neuroimaging under classic psychedelics shows the brain's self-referential control hub (that **default mode network, DMN**) loosening its grip; global connectivity expands; boundaries blur; you *feel* dissolved. Then—baseline returns (Carhart-Harris et al., 2016; Tagliazucchi et al., 2016; Timmermann et al., 2023).

The network re-re-organizes.
The bills still need paying and your mom still has opinions.

Meditation?
Same neighborhood, different street. Seasoned meditators show reduced DMN chatter too—less mind-wandering, less self-story heat.
But again, **it's modulation**, not murder (Brewer et al., 2011; Garrison et al., 2015).

Tools like the **Ego Dissolution Inventory** measure that melted-self feeling. Helpful—but it quantifies a **state**—it doesn't sign any ego's death certificate (Nour et al., 2016; Lynn et al., 2023).

## The Bad Science of "Behead Your Ego"

White-knuckled suppression backfires.

Try not to think of a white bear and you'll conjure a marathon of Christmas polar bears running through your skull.

That rebound shows up across dozens of studies and meta-analyses:

Suppression increases the frequency and intensity of the very thought you're *trying* to bury (Wegner, 1994; Abramowitz et al., 2001; Wang et al., 2020).

**Translation:** declare war on ego and ego drafts you as its publicist.

# Focused Integration

You don't kill it.

You **integrate** it. You **recognize** it. You **listen** for it.

Then you **disobey** it—on purpose, by principle.

## Evidence-based Ego Playbook:

1. **Psychological Flexibility > Self-Annihilation:** ***Acceptance & Commitment Therapy*** (ACT) doesn't tell you to erase your inner voices; it trains you to defuse from them and move toward values. Across disorders and life domains, ACT is as effective as gold-standard treatments—and often better than treatment-as-usual (A-Tjak et al., 2015; Gloster et al., 2020). That is humility in action: "I'm not my thoughts. I'm responsible for my choices."

2. **Self-Compassion as Discipline, Not Dodge:**
If the ego is a brawler, self-compassion is the coach who keeps you in the ring with a plan. Meta-analyses show self-compassion practices reduce depression, anxiety, and stress and improve health behaviors—sleep, exercise, nutrition—aka the unsexy infrastructure of a stable self (Ferrari et al., 2019; Han et al., 2023; Sirois et al., 2015). This isn't coddling. It's the emotional padding that lets you take the punch without quitting—or getting cocky.

3. **Self-Distancing: Talk to Yourself Like a Coach:** Shifting to a fly-on-the-wall vantage ("What does *Jonathan* need to do next?") lowers reactivity and improves problem-solving—even for stress about the *future* (Kross & Ayduk, 2011; White et al., 2019). That's humility again: you are not the center of the storm—you're the sailor reading the wind.

4. **Parts-Work (IFS) to House-Train the Ego:** Instead of exorcising you Ego. Internal Family Systems asks: which *part* is puffing up or panicking?
   You get curious, negotiate, and re-assign roles. Early randomized trials report improvements in pain, depression, and functioning—even in rheumatoid arthritis (Shadick et al., 2013). Not bad for a method that starts with listening instead of lashing.

## Humility:
## The Operating System Upgrade

Humility isn't self-erasure.
It's accurate self-placement.

Research has linked intellectual humility with less polarization and more open-minded, prosocial behavior (Krumrei-Mancuso et al., 2016, 2017; Porter et al., 2022).

Humility predicts generosity, better relationships, and fewer spiritual freak-outs when life punches your theology in the mouth.

It's not meekness; it's *precision* about where you end and reality begins (Exline & Hill, 2012; Grubbs et al., 2014; Tong et al., 2019).

## The Controversial Bit

Psychedelics and deep practice can **open the window** by dampening the brain's self-loop (DMN) and temporarily dissolving boundaries.

Useful.
Sacred, even.

But a new window isn't a new house.

The "ego death" you felt is a postcard from the mountaintop—not your new mailing address (Brewer et al., 2011; Carhart-Harris et al., 2016; Tagliazucchi et al., 2016).

Long-term change comes less from chasing annihilation and more from **daily, humble disobedience** to the ego's impulsive commands—defusion, distance, compassion, values, repetition.If that sounds boring, that's because maturity often is—until your life stops catching fire for dumb reasons. (A-Tjak et al., 2015; Ferrari et al., 2019).

Want a personality movement that *can* stick?
It's not "ego death," it's *openness* after meaning-saturated experiences—and only for some. That change shows up in the literature too, but it's catalyzed by integration and living it out through practice (MacLean et al., 2011; Griffiths et al., 2016).

### In Practice:

**Name the part:** "My Performer is flaring."

**Take altitude:** "What do I do next that serves my calling, not the Pharisee inside me?"

**Act by values:** Tiny, boring, repeatable moves.

**Nightly Review:** "Where did ego try to drive? Where and how did I take the keys back—kindly, firmly?"

You don't kill the ego. You house-train it.
Humility is the leash, not the muzzle.

## The Modern Ego Circus

If you need proof that ego is alive and well, scroll Instagram for 12 seconds.

Whatever the algorithm looks like—
There's a guru for it with all the solutions.

Relationship coaches preaching "Authenticity" with more filters on their Reels than a coffee shop.

TikTok shadow-work experts selling $99 journals like they've got Jung on speed dial.

But look more like an Australian Etsy workbook template with only some of the pages being altered.

Ego thrives in comparison: "I'm better than them" or "I'll never be as good as them."

Same trap.
Same lie.

Social media doesn't create ego.
It amplifies it—like strapping a megaphone to your loudest insecurities.

## Triggers, Teachers, and Taking Ownership

The good news:

**The Ego leaves breadcrumbs.**

Every time you feel jealousy, rage, shame, or any other low-frequency garbage feeling.

That's Ego pointing at something unhealed—and it just got poked.

Jealousy reveals what you secretly want.
Rage reveals a boundary you haven't set.
Shame reveals a festering wound from.

Most people numb these triggers with booze, Netflix, doomscrolling, porn, or worse.

But if you treat those triggers like teachers, they'll guide you straight to what needs healing.

Owning your triggers is biblical too:

***"For every man shall bear his own burden."***
(Galatians 6:5, KJV)

Quit blaming.
Start owning.

# Field Work

**Purpose:** Moving the Ego into the backseat and sitting in the driver's seat.

**Time:** 15 minutes

**Tools:** Pen + paper (or Notes app) + your calendar.

**1) Identify your ego's favorite costume.**
Hero, Martyr, Clown, Chameleon,
Lone Wolf—or your own custom model.
Write it down.

**2) Name the fear underneath.**
Rejection? Being seen? Losing control?
Abandonment? Failure? Success?
Intimacy? Trauma patterns?

**3) Run the seating chart (daily).**
Write one sentence each morning:
Spirit drives when I ________.

Mind navigates by _________.
Ego tries to grab the wheel by _________.

**4) Do one "humble disobedience" rep today.**
Send the message you keep drafting.
Set one boundary.
Tell one trusted person the truth.
Do the two-minute task you keep avoiding.

**5) Nightly keys check.**
Where did ego try to drive today?
Where did you take the keys back?

# Wrapping Up

The ego says: "Don't risk it. Don't even try."

The Spirit says:

***"Have not I commanded thee? Be strong and of a good courage; be not afraid, neither be thou dismayed: for the LORD thy God is with thee whithersoever thou goest."*** (Joshua 1:9, KJV)

And listen—your job isn't to kill your ego.
That's not the assignment.

Your job is to **recognize it**, **laugh at it**, and **choose your Spirit anyway**.

# FVCK UP YOUR EGO

Let me reframe the Ego so you stop treating it like Satan in a pair of skinny jeans.

Because your ego isn't a demon.

Your ego is more like a malfunctioning bodyguard. A scared little bodyguard still reporting threats from ten years ago.

It's *trying* to protect you but it has the emotional intelligence of a drunk racoon with a rape whistle.

It never asks, "Is this true?"
It asks, "Is this safe?"

And the ego's definition of safe is: *don't be seen, don't open up, don't peel the layers back, don't be judged, don't fail publicly, stick with my script; it's fine how it's written.*

Don't just listen and follow blindly.
And don't smack it around like it's a criminal.
Your ego is part of you.
Show it some love and respect.

Ask questions like a loving parent does with a child:

*What are you afraid will happen if I do this?*

*When did you learn to be afraid of this?*

*What's the advantage of obeying you?*

*What's the advantage of disobeying you?*

Your ego usually answers with childlike mathematics:

*If I'm perfect, I'm safe.*

*If I'm liked, I'm safe.*

*If I'm invisible, I'm safe.*

*If I'm safe, I'm safe.*

But you're not *trying* to be safe—
you want peace—
to be free.

So don't "banish" or "murder" your ego. That turns it into a much more powerful villain than before.

Sneakier.
More crafty.
More keen deception.

Even convincing you it's not the one in control—when it is.

Stop allowing a toddler to hold the wheel:
The ego can ride. It cannot drive.

It means well—it just panics loud.

It sees exposure and screams, predator.
It sees possibility and screams, embarrassment.
It sees purpose and screams, risk.

# FVCK UP YOUR EGO

It confuses discomfort with danger.

But the moment you choose Spirit over ego—
You stop shrinking for validation and start carrying presence with confidence.

You stop seeking applause and start walking in purpose.

You stop treating your calling like a hobby and start honoring it like a command.

Your ego wants safety.
Your Spirit wants freedom.

Your ego whispers, "What will they think?"
Your Spirit answers, "Fuck what they think."

Your ego builds walls and calls them protection.
Your Spirit tears them down and calls it resurrection.

So the next time your ego starts screaming in fear—smile at it.

Seriously. A nice warm smile.
Thank it for trying to protect you.
Then name what's actually happening:

"This is fear."
"This is ego."
"This is the old script."
And then choose the new one.

## FVCK IT

Because courage isn't the absence of fear—it's obedience **in the presence** of fear.

It's you taking one step while your ego throws a tantrum in the back seat.

So take its hand. And say: "Remember—you don't drive anymore. My Spirit does."

Then put your eyes back on the road.
Steady the wheel.
And set the cruise.

Because God didn't command you to feel brave.

He commanded you to **be** brave.

# Chapter 3

# Fvck Your Emotions

**Ego Alert:** Your feelings are not prophetic. They're weather predictions with opinions you believe.

**Vow:** I feel it. I name it. I obey my values while I choose my next step.

# The Lie of Feelings

Your emotions are liars.
Not always.
But usually.

Not because you're broken.
Not because emotions are demonic.

But because feelings are terrible **leaders.**

They're biochemical signals—neurotransmitters firing, hormones surging, body sensations your brain is interpreting in fractions of a second, and it pretty much relies on memory for that interpretation.

So if you treat them like absolute truth, they'll own you.
And you will find yourself getting wrecked.

According to science:
Fear isn't a prophecy; it's adrenaline and cortisol lighting up your amygdala like a fire alarm.

Joy isn't divine confirmation; it's dopamine and serotonin after your brain tags something as a win.

Sadness isn't weakness; it's serotonin and norepinephrine bottoming out.

Anger isn't a moral compass; it's a limbic hijack that shoves your prefrontal cortex offline (Davidson, 2000; LeDoux, 1998).

The science is clear: emotions are ***constructed experiences*** (Barrett, 2017).

Because most people don't explode just for being "angry."

They explode because anger was forced to be the only language their nervous system learned to communicate with.

And others don't shut down because they're "fine."

They shut down because they were conditioned to believe feelings are a burden and are best suppressed.

Emotions can be loud. But don't panic.

Loud emotions don't necessarily mean they're dangerous—
although that very well can be—
But loud usually just means **unattended.**

The power move:
When you can feel something fully and still choose wisely on how to act.

That's maturity. That's emotional intelligence.
It's masculine. It's feminine. It's healing.
It's Spirit-led adulthood.

It's not about less emotions.
It's about better **leadership** despite emotions.
The ego side of your brain isn't discovering truth; it's predicting it. And since the ego can only operate within the realms of the

past and future—our emotions are stories. Fables—that your ego tells to explain any sensory input.

And a lot of those stories are pure fucking bullshit.

That's because emotions are incredible servants—
but terrible royalty.
They're not truth—they're weather patterns.

And the weather is very real.
But you don't call a hurricane "part of who you are."

You call it what it is—a hurricane.

And what do we do with hurricanes?

We name them, board up the windows, make smart choices until it passes, and clean up the debris after.

Upgrade the rule thumb:
emotions are ***data***, not ***directives***.

Feel them, name them, respect the signal. But don't worship them—don't give them power.

## Feel It Without Obeying It:

1. **Name it** (1 word): fear, grief, anger, shame, joy.

2. **Locate it** (chest tight? jaw clenched? gut knotted?

3. **Give it a job** that isn't driving.

Do this and you stop letting chemicals control both the gas and the breaks.
Letting your values take the lead.

## The Deceitful Heart

Scripture said this long before neuroscience:

***"The heart is deceitful above all things, and desperately wicked; who can know it?"***
(Jeremiah 17:9, KJV)

Your feelings *will* deceive you—not because they're evil, but because they're **easily hijacked.**

Proverbs 25 backs it up:

***"He that hath no rule over his own spirit is like a city that is broken down, and without walls."***
(Proverbs 25:28, KJV)

If you let emotions run your life, your choices, your actions—you don't have a fortress with secure gates.

Shit you don't even have walls—and every thief, every invader, every demon—every impulse—gets free rein.

You have a fucking dumpster fire with high wind speeds.

So let's nail this home a little more: ***your emotions are not evil—nor invalid—but they are wildly unqualified to lead.***

Let them report. Do not let them rule.

Emotions are **data**, not **directives**. (Yeah—say it again. It's the whole chapter.)

**Gate Protocol:**

1. **Name the feeling** (one word).
2. **Hold the gate** (breathe: 4 count in, 6 count out—three times).
3. **Ask the King** (one-line prayer: *"God, what's the next faithful step?"*).
4. **Act on values, not vibes** (one small step you can do now).

That's how you keep the walls up while your heart calms the fuck down.

## When Emotions Drive

Think of your worst mistakes.
They likely didn't come from a calm, disciplined thought.

They came when emotion grabbed the wheel:

That rage text you shot off at midnight.
The words you screamed at the person you love.
The fight that ended a relationship.
The degree you're still paying off with nothing to show from it.
The resignation you slapped on a desk with no plan.

**Emotion-regulation** research shows that when arousal spikes, limbic circuits (amygdala & friends) downshift the prefrontal cortex—the part of the brain that performs planning, discernment, judgment, long-term thinking, and logic/reason. (Gross, 2002; LeDoux, 1998).

(Think of the movie "Inside Out." Golly, I hope they make another with Riley as an adult. And if you haven't seen both—that's homework for you.)

**Translation:** when you're lit up, your thinking gets dumb and narrow. Your brain trades wisdom for speed and safety. Which explains why we sometimes do or say things we wouldn't have without our emotions leading the front.

So yeah—when you're all high on emotions, you're basically stupid as fuck.

Temporarily. And "temporary" is the key.

## Heat Rules:

**Rule 1: No decisions ≥ 7/10.**
If your intensity is seven or higher, you **do not**: text, post, quit, buy, or confront.

**Rule 2: 4–6 breathing for 60–90s.**
Inhale 4, exhale 6, repeat 6–8 cycles. Longer exhales downshift the body. Decide **after** the downshift.

**Rule 3: HALT check.**
Hungry
Angry
Lonely
Tired.

If yes to any, **pause**. Fix the state, then revisit the matter.

**Rule 4: Write-don't-send.**
I call this "The Lincoln Effect" because I adopted the practice from President Abraham Lincoln. He called the "hot letters." Draft the message. **Do not send.** Sleep on it or set a 24-hour timer.

In practice, I rarely send the first draft. It's come to the point that I'll intentionally use a first draft to get all the emotions out. Then I have the freedom to be past the emotions and focus on writing a fresh one with love, logic, and reason leading the front. Love can land any point.

**Rule 5: Money cooling-off.**
24 hours minimum on big purchases. It would be better not to buy impulsively at all. Let's make sure the big pocket burners are given more attention, time, and awareness.

**Rule 6: One small faithful step.**
When you can't trust your chemistry, trust your **values**: one small action aligned with who you're becoming (drink water,

pray, step outside, apologize for your tone—more content doesn't always help).

### Scripts for the moment you're heated:

**To yourself:** "I'm at an eight. Chemicals first, choices second."
**To the other person:** "I care about this and I'm too hot to be wise. I'll respond tomorrow."
**To your wallet:** "If it's worth buying tomorrow, it will be worth buying after I've slept."

Feel fully.

Act slowly.

When the storm passes (and it will), you'll still have your job, your person, your money—and your dignity.

## Jesus Wept Then Moved

Jesus didn't deny emotions.

He wept at Lazarus's tomb—and then acted (John 11:35–44). When Jesus heard about John the Baptist's death, He withdrew to a desolate place to grieve; the crowds followed, and He turned sorrow into compassion—healing the sick and feeding the five thousand (Matthew 14:13–21).

Paul didn't say "don't get angry." He said:

***"Be ye angry, and sin not: let not the sun go down upon your wrath: Neither give place to the devil."***
(Ephesians 4:26-27, KJV)

In other words: feel it; cage it before it bites; release it before you sleep.

And no—Paul didn't say to bottle it up.
Neither am I.

He said don't sin while angry.

Anger still needs an exit—just one that doesn't hurt people or burn the house down.

**Rule to remember:** emotions are real, not rulers.

Jesus felt deeply and moved faithfully.
Paul admits anger exists and never commands it to open fire.

Feel it fully.
Aim it wisely.
Act from truth with love.

Don't let a 90-second chemical storm create a 90-day shitstorm.

## The 90-Second Rule

Here's a useful reality check: emotions are storms, and storms pass.

Jill Bolte Taylor popularized the idea that the chemical surge of an emotion lasts about **90 seconds**—*if you don't continue to feed it* (Bolte Taylor, 2008).

Ninety fucking seconds.

That's it.
A minute and a half.
It takes longer than that to warm up leftovers in a microwave.

So if your rage lasts hours, if your sorrow lasts weeks, if your fear lasts years.

It's because you keep picking up the damn gift.

Fucking throw it in the fire of yesterday.

You don't need it anymore.
It's not helping you.

## The Scorpion and the Frog

A frog is sitting on a muddy bank.
The river is wide and fast.

Out of the reeds, a scorpion crawls forward with his stinger glinting with death.

"Carry me across," the scorpion pleads.

The frog recoils. "You'll sting me."

The scorpion tilts its head—logic dripping from its voice.

"If I sting you, I drown too. Why would I kill us both?"

Against all instinct, the frog agrees.

Halfway across, the scorpion sinks its stinger deep into the frog.

As venom floods his body, the frog gasps, "Why? Now we both die."

And the scorpion whispers: "Because it is my nature."

That's your emotions when they're in charge.

They promise they'll behave.

They promise logic.

They promise they'll help.

Then you trust them—and then they sting.
Almost every fucking time.

So what do you do when emotions—yours or theirs—come at you with teeth gnashing, stingers stinging, and pinchers pinching?

One option is certain—you don't have to carry them across the river.

## The Samurai's Gift

One day a samurai walks through the market. A madman rushes at him, spitting curses—coward, dog, disgrace.

Crowds gather, waiting for certain bloodshed.

The samurai stood like a mountain.
Calm. Silent. Unbothered.

The madman became tired and stormed off with rage still burning in his chest. A villager asked, "Why did you not strike? He insulted your honor!"

The samurai said, "If someone offers you a gift, and you refuse it, to whom does the gift belong?"

The giver.

That's what emotions can be: gifts you don't have to accept.

They belong to whoever tries to hand them to you.

No reaction is *often* the best reaction.

Parables teach the correct move.

Scripture shows us the cost of emotional slavery.

## Lot's Wife and Samson

Lot's wife was told to flee and not look back. She let longing rule her heart. She turned her gaze back on Sodom—and turned into salt (Genesis 19:26).

Samson—mighty in strength—destroyed by *his* lust. He let Delilah's seduction blind him until he was chained, humiliated, and literally blinded (Judges 16).

Two people undone not by armies.
Not by fate.

By emotions they refused to master.

**Bottom line:** Feel everything. Obey nothing until it aligns with truth, value, and God's voice.

## History Testifies

Scripture shows the cost of obeying the feels. History also shows the power of choosing **values**.

***"Between stimulus and response, there is a space. In that space is our power to choose our response."***
- often attributed to Vikto Frankl

Viktor Frankl was an Austrian Holocaust survivor—in Auschwitz. He watched men being stripped of *everything* during World War II.

Family. Dignity. Freedom. Even gold teeth.

Yet he discovered the final freedom: choice.

If a man in a death camp can choose meaning over despair, you can choose discipline when traffic cuts you off.

Or look at **Jackie Robinson** in 1947–

Stadiums booed, racial slurs thrown between pitches aimed at his chin, spikes came in high. Every emotion in his body could've justified swinging back.

He made a different move: **restraint with purpose**.

He let his love and skill for the game speak for him and refused to let rage run his mouth or his actions.

That wasn't pretending feelings weren't real.
It was deciding they didn't get to hold the mic.

## Weapons of Emotional Mastery

**Pause** – When the storm rises, breathe. Deep breathing calms cortisol, activates the parasympathetic system, and reboots your nervous system (Jerath et al., 2006).

**Name It** – Say, "This is fear. This is anger." Labeling emotions dampens amygdala activation (Lieberman et al., 2007).

**Reframe It** – Pain isn't punishment; it's training. Rejection isn't failure; it's redirection. Psychologists call it *cognitive reappraisal* (Gross, 2002).

**Choose Values Over Feelings** – Ask, "What would the best version of me do right now?" Then do that, whether or not you feel like it.

# Field Work: Emotional TSA

**Purpose:** Feel everything. Obey nothing until it aligns with truth, values, and God's voice.

**Time:** 12–18 minutes

**Tools:** Phone timer + Notes app (or paper) + calendar

## Step 1 – Build Your "Heat Scale"

**Right now, write:**
"When I'm emotional, I'm not 'bad.' I'm just lit up."

**Then set your rule:** "No decisions at 6/10 or higher."

(That means: no texting, posting, quitting, buying, or confronting, nothing.)

## Step 2 – The Gate Protocol

Run this exactly as written—this is your "don't burn the house down" sequence:

1. **Name it (one word):** ______

2. **Hold the gate:** breathe 4 in/6 out (3 rounds)

3. **Ask the King (one line):** "God, what's the next step you need me to take?"

4. **Act on values, not vibes:** one small step you can do now.

## Step 3 — The 90-Second Timer

Set a timer for **90 seconds**.

For that full 90 seconds, you do **nothing** except breathe and let the wave pass.

**Reminder:** the chemical surge is short—what makes it last is you feeding it.

## Step 4 — Choose One "Heat Rule" You'll Actually Use

Pick **one** and write it as a personal law:

**4–6 breathing**

**HALT check (Hungry/Angry/Lonely/Tired)**

**Write-don't-send + sleep on it**

**Cooling-off rule (24 hours for purchases)**

**One small faithful step**

## Step 5 — Pre-write Your "Hot Scripts"

Copy/paste these somewhere you can grab fast:

To yourself: **"I'm at an eight. Chemicals first, choices second."**

To them: **"I care about this and I'm too hot to be wise. I'll respond tomorrow."**

To your wallet: **"If it's worth buying today, it'll be worth buying after I've slept."**

### Receipts:

Take a screenshot of your Notes titled: **"Emotions = Data"**and set ONE calendar reminder labeled: **"Hold the Gate (4–6)"**

### Reflection:

Where am I letting "heat" make choices my future self has to clean up?

## Wrapping Up

The brutal truth in this chapter: emotions aren't going away.

You can't kill them. You can't pray them away. You can't positive-think them into eternal silence.

They're part of your divine design. God gave you emotions.

They were just never meant to be your master; they were meant to be your messenger.
But most people don't believe they even have a choice.

We worship our emotions like they're idols.

We let them dictate our choices, our moods, our relationships, even our faith. We build entire lives around how we *feel*—then wonder why we're never stable.

You can't build a kingdom on shifting sand. And emotions? They'll sink you like quicksand.

Let's get one thing straight: the point of this chapter wasn't to make you cold or becoming forever detached.

It was meant to wake you up.

Feeling deeply isn't the same as living wisely.

Please—feel everything. It's important. The pain. The rage. The lust. The jealousy. The loneliness. Even euphoria. And joy. And pleasure. And love.

But learn to feel *without* acting with your feels.

That's emotional maturity. That's spiritual mastery—real emotional intelligence.

So **fuck your emotions**—not in hatred, but in hierarchy. You're not erasing them; you're re-ordering their priority.

You're reclaiming your throne.

Because anger can become courage.
Fear can become awareness.
Sorrow can become compassion.
Even guilt can become conviction—if the Spirit translates it.

But if you don't?

Those same emotions will turn on you—they'll become parasitic.

They feed on your peace and poison your purpose.

They whisper love songs that lead you into lust traps.
They nudge you toward revenge and call it justice.
They tell you you're "following your heart," when really you're following your wounds.

Unchecked emotion will crown you tonight and crucify you in the morning.

So dethrone them.

They are not kings.

They are not prophets.

They are not God.

***"For God hath not given us the spirit of fear; but of power, and of love, and of a sound mind."***
(2 Timothy 1:7, KJV)

That's the truth.
That's part of the freedom you're chasing.

The day you stop letting emotions drive you is the day you finally taste what it means to be free from their clutch.

Emotions are signals—but you are the interpreter.

You are the gatekeeper.

Your limbic system **(the emotional center)** fires first—raw, fast, reactive. But the prefrontal cortex—your God-given higher-order of reasoning—is the throne room.

The real control room.

Every time you pause before reacting, you strengthen that circuit. That's neuroplasticity—**brain training**.

The world says, “Follow your heart.”

God says:

***“Keep thy heart with all diligence; for out of it are the issues of life.”*** (Proverbs 4:23, KJV)

The heart feels before it discerns.

Think of Jesus in Gethsemane—sweating blood, overwhelmed with sorrow. He didn’t pretend He wasn’t afraid. He felt it—but He didn’t follow it.

He said:

***“Saying, Father, if thou be willing, remove this cup from me: nevertheless not my will, but thine, be done.”*** (Luke 22:42, KJV)

That’s the model.

Not emotional suppression—**emotional submission.**

Submitting emotion to the Spirit.
Letting your feelings kneel before your faith.

Because emotion might tell you what’s true now.

But wisdom tells you what’s true eternally.

So the next time your emotions flare—when anger surges, loneliness aches, or fear whispers "you're not enough;" take a breath.

Smile, even.
And remind your soul who's in charge.

*"You don't own me anymore. You don't run me anymore. You can ride in the back next to Mr. Ego. I'm driving now."*

Freedom isn't the absence of emotion—it's the mastery of it.

And the moment you learn to master what once mastered you...that's some real renovating of the soul.

Now we deal with the next liar that loves to sit on your throne.

# Chapter 4

# Fvck Motivation

**Ego Alert:** Constantly looking for motivation is how people die average.

**Vow:** I will not rely on hype. I will set and keep standards. I will do all the reps.

## The Flakiest Friend You've Got

Motivation is another liar we wrongfully trust and depend on.

A loud, unreliable, smooth-talking hype man who shows up when the drinks are flowing and the music's loud—then ghosts you the second you actually need him.

He's the friend who hypes you at midnight:
*"I'm locked in bro! We're running at 6 a.m. bro! We're gonna crush it!"*

Where is he when your alarm goes off?

Snoring. Hungover. Fucking MIA.

Now you're staring at your sneakers feeling like a fucking idiot. ("Go for the run he said. It'll be fun he said.")

For fuck's sake—please—stop trusting motivation.

Stop expecting it to just be there.
Stop searching for it.
Stop chasing it.

Just fucking stop.
I see it everywhere.

Motivation this and motivation that.
Motivation is **not** your ride-or-die.
He's nowhere close to reliable or consistent.

He's the flaky dude who bails on moving day but texts you that same evening wanting to grab a beer.

Motivation is spark.

***Discipline*** is fire.

Discipline is the friend who shows up quietly, takes out the trash, pays the bills, and doesn't need applause for doing basic shit we know we should do anyway.

If you want to win at anything—your health, your relationships, your walk with God—you need **loyalty**, not hype.

Motivation is a **mood**—a feeling—a dopamine pop from novelty, a story your brain tells when conditions feel perfect.

Then it rains.
You're fatigued.
Life starts throwing junk balls.

And your hype man disappears while excuses (hello again, Ego) starts clucking like chickens during a thunderstorm.

That's why *"I'll do it when I feel like it"* is just procrastination dressed in its Sunday best.

**Truth**: Feelings fluctuate. Design doesn't.

Stop asking, *"Do I feel like it?"*

Start asking, *"What did I decide?"*

Stop asking, *"How do I get motivated?"*

Start asking, *"What do I do even when I'm not motivated?"*

Here's another fun story as a fun way to differentiate discipline from motivation. As well as the consequences of each.

## The Ants and the Grasshopper

It's Summer in the fields. Green grass. Long sunny days.

A grasshopper leaps through the grass, singing, enjoying the breeze, and living like winter is a mythical illusion. Nearby, ants march in lines, dragging grains of wheat back to their hill.

"Why work so hard?" the grasshopper laughs. "Come sing with me! There's plenty of food, plenty of time."

The ants didn't stop. "Winter is coming," they said. "We're preparing."

Day after day, the ants toiled.
Day after day, the grasshopper sang and danced.

Then winter comes. The fields go bare. The wind cut like knives. The grasshopper shivers, starving, and stumbles to the ant hill begging for food. But the ants closed the door and the grasshopper died.

Motivation is the grasshopper—loud when it's easy, useless when it's hard.

Discipline is the ant—boring, steady, but alive after the storm hits.

***"Go to the ant, thou sluggard; consider her ways, and be wise;"*** (Proverbs 6:6, KJV)

## The Spark vs. The Fire

Psychologists define motivation as "the process that initiates, guides, and sustains goal-directed behavior" (Ryan & Deci, 2000).

Sounds neat.
But here's the real deal: **motivation is a spark, not a fire.**

Imagine you're stranded in the woods.
You've got one match. Strike it and...spark.

That's motivation. You can see the light but you're still cold. And if you don't feed it with kindling and logs, it dies out—quick. And you're left shivering while wolves circle your camp.

**Discipline is the firewood.**

The gathering.

The preparation.

The tending.

The stoking.

It's repetitive.
It's unsexy.
But it's what keeps you alive when the spark is gone.

***"In all labour there is profit: but the talk of the lips tendeth only to penury."*** (Proverbs 14:23, KJV)

Motivation talks.
Discipline toils.

Guess which one pays off?

## The Wise and Foolish Builders

Jesus told a story that nails this difference (Matthew 7:24–27).
Was He was talking about motivation and discipline?
Not likely—but the dots still connect the same.

One man built his house on rock. He dug deep, set the foundation, and worked steadily.

Another man built on sand; fast, easy, exciting.

Then the storms came.

Rain poured. Rivers rose.
The wind whipped.

The house on rock stood.
The house on sand collapsed.

Motivation builds shit on sand; quick results with a weak foundation.

Discipline builds on rock: slow, difficult—but unshakable.

Not convinced?

Don't want to take God's advice?

Cool—

but science agrees with God's Word.

## The Science of Why Motivation Fucks You Over

Here's why motivation can't be trusted: **it's chemically built to fade.**

Motivation is tightly linked to dopamine—the brain's reward-pursuit chemical.

Kent C. Berridge (2007) showed that dopamine isn't really about *liking* the reward; it's about *wanting* it.

Every time you imagine something shiny—six-pack abs, a new business, financial freedom—your brain can spike dopamine in *anticipation*, not celebration. (Schultz, 2016; Montague, Hyman, & Cohen, 2004).

That rush makes starting something feel—electric.

**But there's the trap:**
The same circuitry lights up when your phone pings, your DMs flash, or someone likes your post.

Tiny cues.
Tiny hits.
Repeat forever.

Engineered to trigger micro-bursts of dopamine. And those loops overlap with addictive behavior patterns (Volkow, Wang, Fowler, Tomasi, & Telang, 2011).

As Adam Alter (2017) explains, our devices are designed to keep us hooked on that chemical loop.

It's not exactly the same as hitting a crack pipe, but neurologically, the pattern is familiar: cue, anticipation, hit, repeat.

The feeling fades, and you're left chasing the next buzz.

That's why motivation dies.
It's attached to dopamine.

And it's when dopamine dips that motivation ghosts the fuck out of you.

Then there's willpower research: Baumeister's ego depletion model suggested that self-control functions like a muscle—push it too hard, and it gets tired (Baumeister et al., 1998).

While later research debated its limits; the lived truth remains obvious: **willpower burns out fast when it's your *only* fuel**.

Discipline doesn't depend on hype or mood.
Discipline is a value.
A system.
A standard.

That's what most aren't willing to accept.

It's not glamorous.

Ironically, this is where real, sustainable, results happen.

## Culture's Addiction to Fast Results

We're living in a world that wants results now, but rarely does anyone want to work for the results.

As a result we have thousands of gurus selling you bullshit hacks, scams, conflicting information, and sugar-pill supplements.

We get endless "programs" with bold punchlines and a hard stop date.

The real issue: **Anything designed with an end will end.**

Results included.

Then what?

No direction.
No continuation.

Most people fall right back into the lifestyle they had before the challenge. Often—from my experience—people end up in worse physical shape than before.

***"Now no chastening for the present seemeth to be joyous, but grievous: nevertheless afterward it yieldeth the peaceable fruit of righteousness unto them which are exercised thereby."***
(Hebrews 12:11, KJV)

Motivation bails on you.
Discipline bears you fruit.

If you still think motivation will carry you, let's take a field trip in January.

## Resolution Disillusion

The gyms in January are packed wall-to-wall with resolution warriors—nuts to butts around the weights, treadmills, hashtags and selfies everywhere: **#NewYearNewMe**

Fast-forward to February: the gym is nearly fucking empty.
All the hype. All the intention. All the fluffed egos.

Ghosts.

Motivation came in hot; then sore muscles met cold mornings, and it peaced the fuck out.

Discipline is why the lifers are still there in April...

July...
October...on Christmas Day.

Discipline doesn't negotiate.

***"I have fought a good fight, I have finished my course, I have kept the faith:"*** (2 Timothy 4:7, KJV)

Notice: Paul didn't say, *"I stayed motivated."*
He said he finished.
He said he kept faith.

This isn't just a theory.

I've watched motivation vanish and discipline rebuild the house—again and again.

## Stories From the Trenches

Sarah wanted to lose thirty pounds.

Week one: perfect meal prep, six workouts, daily tracking.
Motivation had her flying—*Let's. Fucking. Go*

Week three: sick kids, work stress, missed one workout—then two. "Screw it, I'll start again Monday." Monday never came. Motivation ghosted.

I knocked on her door.
I brought her family in.
We talked it out.

She needed more support at home, real accountability, and **minimum standards**: three workouts per week, protein at every meal, a ten-minute walk daily.

**A baseline minimum.**
Flexible.
Realistic.
Baby steps.

Non-negotiable.

Do it tired.
Do it stressed.
Do it pissed the fuck off.

Bad days.

Great days.

The (eventual) result?

She didn't just lose weight. She gained consistency, freedom, confidence—and a whole lot of strength.

**Then there was Jake.**

Different goals—similar mindset.
He was a bit scrawny, but fully hyped, yelling "Let's goooo!" after every set.

Two weeks in:
still no washboard abs,
his spirit crushed,
he's ready to quit.

What saved him wasn't more hype.

It was boring structure:
**Lift.**
**Eat.**
**Sleep.**
**Repeat.**

Jake's non-negotiables didn't match Sarah's;
and so yours will be yours.
Create them.

***"But be ye doers of the word, and not hearers only, deceiving your own selves."*** (James 1:22, KJV)

Sarah and Jake transformed from **hearers** (motivated) to **doers** (disciplined).

## The Hare vs. The Tortoise

The hare sprinted with swagger, bragged mid-race, and even had the audacity to take a fucking nap.

The tortoise plodded—slow, steady—and crossed the line while the hare was still rubbing the sleep from his eyes.

**Motivation** is the hare: flashy, overconfident, inconsistent.

**Discipline** is the tortoise: humble, a little slow, victorious nonetheless.

Here's one more picture you can't argue with. This one doesn't come from a fable. It comes from a living legend.

## Michael Jordan's Flu Game

Game 5, 1997 NBA Finals. Jordan had the flu—fever, exhaustion, no motivation. He played 44 minutes, dropped 38 points, and carried the Bulls to the win.

That wasn't motivation.
That was the ***identity*** of discipline saying,

*"I'm the guy who shows up."*

***"And let us not be weary in well doing: for in due season we shall reap, if we faint not."***
(Galatians 6:9, KJV)

# Motivation's Deception

Motivation always sells the same garbage:

- "Start fresh Monday."
- "You deserve a break."
- "Skip one day—no big deal."
- "Go big or go home."

I've watched it for years: one skipped day becomes two, then a week, then "We'll take the summer off; it's so busy."

That's not "life"; that's the lie.

"Go big or go home" burns you out.

**Motivation** sets you up for guilt, shame, lies, and quitting.

**Discipline** tells a simple truth: "It doesn't matter if you want to or not. This is what we're doing."

And when motivation fails?

The algorithm has a product ready.

## Discipline: The Unsexy Superpower

Search **"Top 10 hacks to stay motivated"** and you'll find influencers sipping $12 energy drinks, journaling on aesthetic notepads, selling bootcamps promising "limitless motivation."

Bullshit.

Motivation hacks are espresso shots—rush, crash, repeat.

Real change doesn't come from hacks. It comes from habits—discipline on autopilot:

**Charles Duhigg:** cues → routines → rewards form habits (Duhigg, 2012).

**James Clear:** tiny habits compound into massive identity shifts (Clear, 2018).

Motivation is sexy.
Discipline is dull as fuck.

No one is posting viral TikToks about flossing or drinking enough water.

But boring ***wins***.

Every.
Single.
Time.

Discipline is showing up when you don't want to.

It's doing alllll the reps when nobody's watching.

Over time, discipline *becomes* a part of your identity.

Now we make it livable.

## Building Discipline Without Burning Out

**Set minimum standards:**
Forget perfect.

Do the bare minimum—**consistently**.
Three workouts. Ten-minute walks. A gallon of water daily.

**Stack wins:**
Every promise you keep builds identity.
Small wins **compound** into confidence.

**Detach from feelings:**
Don't feel like it?
Too bad. Do it anyway.

("Painful now, peaceful later.")

**Rewrite your self-talk:**
When ego says, "Skip it."
Answer back, "Nope. This is who I am now."

**Shift identity:**
Don't "*try.*" **Be.** (Foreshadowing)

Motivation talks.
**Discipline acts.**

This is where Scripture and science shake hands.

Psychology calls it **self-determination theory** (Ryan & Deci, 2000): when you act from internal identity and values, you stick with it. The Bible calls it obedience and faithfulness.
Same truth, different language.

## Field Work: Discipline Blueprint

**Day 1: Choose your minimum standard (non-negotiable)**
Pick one domain to start: body, money, craft, faith, relationship. Write a minimum you can do even on your worst day (10 minutes, one page, one walk, one prayer, one budget line item).

**Day 2: Pre-decide your time + trigger**
"When I finish ____, I do ____."
(Example: "After coffee, I walk 10 minutes.")

**Day 3: Remove one friction point**
Shoes by the door.
Food prepped.
App deleted.

**Day 4: Add one accountability point**
Text a friend: "Minimum standard is ____.
I'll check in at ___."
No TED Talk. Just a timestamp.

**Day 5: Practice doing it ugly**
Do the minimum while tired, annoyed, bored.
Prove you don't need the mood.

**Day 6: Miss-proof your plan**
Write your rule: "If I miss, I do the minimum the next day—no shame spiral." Discipline isn't perfection. It's recovery speed.

**Day 7: Review + lock identity**
Finish this sentence: "I'm not someone who relies on motivation. I'm someone who ____."

# Wrapping Up

Motivation is a spark of ignition.
Discipline is the roaring fire.

And fire is what keeps you alive when the night gets cold.

Most people keep *trying* to stay warm off of sparks alone.

They strike match after match—new playlist, new quote, new "Monday reset," new guru, new motivational speaker—then the first wind shows up: stress, fatigue, feelings...*pffft*.

Darkness returns.
And that's when the spiral starts.

You don't just miss the workout—you start doubting yourself. You don't just fall off the plan—you question whether you're even built for follow-through.

That's the hidden cost of chasing motivation: it turns a normal human emotion into a character indictment.

But the truth is simpler—and way more savage:

Motivation fades when the crowd stops clapping.
Discipline endures when nobody's watching.

Motivation thrives on dopamine.
Discipline thrives on commitment.

Motivation is a feeling.
Discipline is a decision.

Your life cannot be built on feelings.

Feelings are weather. Weather changes. And most people let weather make the executive decisions.

So stop asking, "Do I feel like it?"
Start asking, "What did I pre-decide?"

Pre-decision is holy.
Pre-decision is grown.

Pre-decision is how you stop negotiating with yourself like you're two different people in a toxic relationship.

Discipline is you deciding—*ahead of time*—who you are, what you do, and what you don't do...then showing up to honor that decision long after the mood left the room.

Motivation is cheap.
Discipline is costly.

But the reward of discipline is freedom—real freedom.
The kind that shows up when you can finally trust yourself again.

Your greatest breakthroughs don't happen on your best days. They happen on the days you don't feel like showing up—when your body says no and your spirit says go.

That's where transformation lives: repetition.

Quiet obedience.
The unglamorous rep that never trends.
And yeah—obedience...

***"Now no chastening for the present seemeth to be joyous, but greivous: nevertheless afterward it yieldeth the peaceable fruit of righteousness unto them which are exercised thereby."***
(Hebrews 12:11, KJV)

Pain now, peace later.
Suffering now, strength later.
Discipline now, fruit later.

Discipline isn't punishment—it's preparation.

Because motivation is chemically built to disappear.
Dopamine loves anticipation, not consistency.

If you depend on hype, you're trying to heat your house with fireworks—loud, flashy, gone in a blink.

And when motivation fails, culture has an offer: a hack, a shortcut, a quick fix.

Bullshit.

Real change comes from habits—discipline on autopilot.

Not "try harder."
**Build smarter.**

Make it livable, not perfect:

**Set minimum standards.**

**Stack small wins.**

**Detach from feelings.**

**Rewrite your self-talk: "Nope. This is who I am now."**

Because once discipline becomes identity, debate dies.

When you stop saying, "I'm trying," and start saying, "I am," the back door closes.

Discipline is not self-hatred.
Discipline is self-respect.

It's you refusing to abandon **Future You** for the comfort of **Present You**.

So when your brain screams, "I don't feel like it," smile—and move anyway.
Transformation doesn't crash in with trumpets; it sneaks up through small, daily acts of faithfulness.

Motivation is fleeting.
Discipline endures.

Motivation ignites.
Discipline sustains.

So light your fire.
Feed it daily.

**Protect it fiercely.**

Because sparks fade— but the disciplined burn forever.
And if that line scares you a little?
Good.

Next chapter we kill the cutest lie of all.

# Chapter 5

# Fvck Trying

**Ego Alert:** "I'll try" is a coward's emergency exit cosplaying as honest effort.

**Vow:** When I commit. I do. Period.

## Loophole of Effort

Two infamous words almost every human has said before attempting...well, anything:

**"I'll try."**

What the fuck are we "trying," exactly?

Better question: **What do we want—bad enough to commit?**

Because "try" isn't honest effort. It's a hedge.
It's a mental escape hatch you install *before* you even start.

The thing most people miss?
**How you talk to yourself shapes what you tolerate from yourself.**

Psychologists have found that the language we use can change how our brains frame commitment.

In a set of experiments, people who framed goals in definite action terms (**"I will"**) were significantly more likely to follow through than those using tentative terms (**"I'll try"**) (Ludwig, Srivastava, and Berkman, 2018).

**Translation:** "Try" keeps the back door open."Do" shuts and locks that door. "Trying" is often procrastination wearing a halo.

It sounds holy.
It feels humble.

But it keeps you from the one thing that actually changes a life: **commitment with a clock.**

Trying says: "I'll do it when life cooperates."
Doing says: "I'm doing it even if life throws chairs at me from across the room."

Make it measurable.
Give it edges.

Not "I'll try to read more."
"I'll read ten pages a day. No debate."

Not "I'll try to get healthier."
"Proein with every meal. Water before coffee. Walk after dinner."

Trying is emotional.
Doing is procedural.

And when you fail—and you will—you don't say, "Ope. Welp. I tried. See? I can't do it."

You say, "That way didn't work. What data do I have? What adjustments can be made? Let's continue."

So here's the rule for the rest of your life:

If it matters.
You don't ***"try."***

You fucking **do**, or you fucking **don't**.

## Yoda Was Right

Luke Skywalker's X-wing is sunk in the swamps of Dagobah. Yoda tells him to lift it with the Force.

Luke groans: "Alright, I'll try."

He scrunches his face, stretches out his hand, and half-heartedly pushes. The ship wobbles, starts to rise... then crashes back down. He pants through saying "I can't. It's too big."

Yoda's response is the most savage mic drop in cinematic history: **"Do. Or do not. There is no try."**

Luke didn't fail because the Force failed him.
He failed because his heart wasn't all-in.

That's what "try" is: **pre-quit language.**
Scripture spits the same vibe; without the green alien:

***"But let your communication be, Yea, yea; Nay, nay: for whatsoever is more than these cometh of evil."*** (Matthew 5:37, KJV)

**Make it binary:**

- Replace "I'll try" with "I will" or "I won't."
- Name the first action (one concrete step).
- Do it now, or schedule it—no third option.

# The Fuck Trying Philosophy

Now that I'm typing this out, I imagine the Nike slogan team back in the 80s:

"We've been trying boss! We can't think of anything catchy."

"No, Bob, that's unacceptable...I need this done...Just do it."

(Probably not how it went. But still.)

If the slogan had been "Just Try It," they wouldn't be Nike. Or at least not the Nike we know today.

Definitely not as much as "Just Do It."

"Try" is limp."Do" is power.

My "fuck trying" philosophy didn't come from Nike though. Or even Scripture to be honest. It came from music.

In the early 2000s, Slightly Stoopid's *"Everything You Need"* hit me with lyrics that tattooed themselves onto my brain. (I'm not able to quote lyrics for legal reasons but you'll know it when you hear it.)

The lyrics you'll hear put words into a lesson I learned early in life without knowing it until the song came into my world.

It started in baseball—a year or two into my traveling team. I noticed one day—one of those light bulb moments.

The harder I *tried* to hit a home run—the more likely I was to strike out or hit an easy pop fly. But when I stepped into the batter's box fully relaxed, thoughtless, and just swung?

That's when baseballs got lost, windshields were broken, and infielders learned what fear actually is.

When I tried, I failed, sometimes hard.
And the harder I tried, the more likely I was to fail hard.
When I stopped "trying" and started ***doing***, things clicked.

One real move beats a thousand maybes.

## The Cat and the Fox

A fox strutted through the woods like he owned the place—tail high, chest puffed—bragging to a cat about how clever he was.

"I've got a thousand tricks," the fox said. "A thousand ways to outsmart the hunters."

The cat tilted his head. Calm. Unimpressed."I've only got one," the cat said. "But it's enough."

The fox rolled his eyes. "One trick? That's pathetic. I could teach you a few..."

Before the fox could finish his TED talk, shouts rippled through the trees—hounds barking, hunters closing in.

The cat didn't hesitate. One fluid move, he dug his claws into the bark and shot up a tree—safe on a high branch. His heart pounding but alive.

The fox darted left. Then right. Dig a hole? Play dead? Run in circles? Trick one, two, three...ten—his mind rifled through options like a gambler flipping cards. Indecision slowed his feet.

The hounds caught him. Teeth, fur, blood.
His thousand tricks meant nothing.

That's you when you stall—collecting "options" while time bleeds.

**It's better to have one solid action than a thousand things to "try."**

As the line often attributed to Bruce Lee goes:
**"I fear not the man who has practiced 10,000 kicks once, but the man who has practiced one kick 10,000 times."**

Scripture is blunt about it:

***"A double minded man is unstable in all his ways."***
(James 1:8, KJV)

Stop chasing clever.
Stop rummaging through options and outcomes.

Commit.
Then fucking do the damned thing.

Because from fables to bumper stickers—the message hasn't changed, but the slogan has been sabotaging you.

## Try, Try, and Try Again...

***"If at first you don't succeed, try, try again."***

Teachers drilled it.
Coaches shouted it.
Parents embroidered it on shirts.

The flaw is subtle: **"try again" trains hesitation.**

It puts the focus on attempting rather than committing.

You burn more energy deciding whether or not you're still in it than actually being in it.

That's why so many of us are exhausted.

We're not failing because we aren't capable.
We're failing because we've conditioned ourselves to live in a perpetual loop of 'try, try again."

Jesus cuts through it with a parable that smacks "trying" right in the mouth (Matthew 21:28–32).

## The Two Sons

A father told the first son, "Go work in the vineyard today."

The son snapped back, “I will not.”

But later, the son's conscience poked at him. He changed his mind and went to work.

The father told the second son the same.
This son smiled, “I go, sir.”

But he never went.

Jesus asked, “Which of the two did the will of his father?”

The answer was obvious: the one who went to work despite what was said.

Words are cheap.
Promises are dead air in a balloon that needs helium.

Action ***is*** the receipt.
And Scripture in James hammers this truth home:

***“But be ye doers of the word, and not hearers only, deceiving your own selves.”*** (James 1:22, KJV)

## What I Don’t Mean by “Fuck Trying”

Let me be absolutely clear—because somebody is going to hear what they want—even if they have to twist my message.

I mean people do it with the Bible and claim righteousness—why would my book be any different?

So this is to reduce any contortion of the message I'm relaying to you:
I'm not saying "don't work hard."
I'm not saying "be lazy."

I'm not saying "quit when it's tough."

I'm saying: ***trying* is half-assery. *Doing* is whole...assery.**

Carol Dweck's work nailed this home in her research on growth mindset.

In one famous study, kids were given impossible puzzles. Some quit immediately, saying, "I tried." Others leaned in, saying, "I love a challenge." (Dweck, C.S., 2006)

Guess which kids grew, learned, and eventually solved real problems?

Yeah, the ones who treated effort and failure as part of the process. The doing.

A growth mindset isn't about "trying harder."
It's about ***committing to do until you learn.***

Ecclesiastes puts skin in the game:

***"Whatsoever thy hand findeth to do, do it with thy might; for there is no work, nor device, nor knowledge, nor wisdom, in the grave, whither thou goest."*** (Ecclesiastes 9:10, KJV)

Notice: ***do***.
Not *try*.

You don't "try" to get your oil changed when it needs to be changed. You go get the fucking oil changed.

Same applies with anything that matters—like the gym—or rather the results you want from the gym.

They don't appear from trying.
They are the product of what you do.

What did most kids look forward to most in elementary school?

Gym class or recess.

As adults, a lot of us have stapled a stack of failed goals to the gym door, so walking in no longer feels like recess; it feels like regret.

I want to hammer it in a little more:
**Consistent execution of your non-negotiables will make it happen.**

Which brings us to another fable favorite of mine.

# The Bamboo Tree

We just talked about doing vs. dabbling. Here's the picture that makes it unforgettable.

Picture this: you're a farmer in China.

You plant a bamboo seed in the ground.

You water it. You fertilize it.
(You even talk to it if you're a little weird like me.)

And then—nothing.

A month goes by—still nothing.
A year—just dirt.

Two years—same damn patch of nothing.

Three years—you start to wonder if you're the biggest fool alive, wasting time on a seed that doesn't give a shit about you.

Four years—what in the actual fuck?

Then, in year five—BAM!
Shoots rocket out of the ground, climbing as much as 80 feet in only a few weeks.

**Now the question:**
Did the bamboo grow 80 feet in a few weeks...or five years?

The truth? Five years.

The whole time, under the soil, it was putting down roots—deep, deep—roots.

Strong roots.

A foundation that can support insane growth.

If the farmer had said, “Eh, I’ll try for a couple years and see what happens,” he’d have walked away before the miracle ever showed.

This is life.
This is the gym.
This is your marriage.
This is your calling.

You don’t “try” for a little while and quit when nothing looks different.

You do.
You commit.
You water.
You show up.

Because growth is happening underground even when your eyes can’t see it.

Scripture gives the same instruction:

***"And let us not be weary in well doing: for in due season we shall reap, if we faint not."***
(Galatians 6:9, KJV)

Not if we try.
Not if we dabble.

If we do not give up.
If we continue to do—we reap the fruit of the harvest.

Consistency, like discipline, isn't sexy.
But it's the undefeated champion of the world.

Keep watering.
Keep showing up.

Your bamboo shoots are coming.

**Root Work:**

**Name the seed:** one concrete aim (marriage check-in, Psalm a day, 10-minute walk).

**Name the water:** one daily action (text, read, move).

**Name the season:** give it **at least six weeks** before you judge the soil.

## The Try Trap

"Trying" is the cleanest way to stay stuck while still feeling like a good person.

It's the language of **pre-excuses:**

**"I'll try to go to the gym."** (*unless I don't feel like it.*)

**"I'll try to be consistent."** (*unless life happens... which it will.*)

**"I'll try to stop doing that."** (*unless it's uncomfortable.*)

And here's the part nobody admits:

**"Try" is often how you avoid the shame of saying no.**

Because **"no"** is honest.

**"Try"** lets you look committed while staying uncommitted.

So I'm taking the word away.
If you're in, say yes—then act.

If you're out, say no—and stop dragging the goal behind you like a dead deer.

**Trying is drifting.**
**Doing is direction.**
Now let's turn direction into a system

## Break the Loop: Commit Protocol

The fix for "try mode" isn't more hype.

It's **pre-deciding.**

Research on implementation intentions show how simple plans—"If X, then I do Y"—increase follow-through across a wide range of behaviors (Gollwitzer & Sheeran, 2006).

Why?

Because **if-then shuts the back door that "try" leaves cracked open.**

The language you use matters too.
Not language like English or Spanish language.

I mean the words you choose to speak—they matter.

A small shift in framework will shape your identity into a decision maker rather than the debater, which helps you stick to your commitments (Patrick & Hagtvedt, 2012).

Here's the **Commitment Protocol**.

Steal it, use it—don't just admire it.
I also followed it with some examples of "if-then" framing:

### 1) Replace "try" with a commitment sentence

"I'll try to work out." → **"At 7:00 p.m., after dishes, I will walk 10 minutes."**

"I'll try to eat better." → **"At lunch, I will eat 30g of protein first and then one cup of broccoli."**

## 2) Add an if–then trigger (shuts the back door)

**If** it's 7:00 p.m., **then** shoes on and out the door.

**If** coffee is brewing, **then** I read one Psalm.

## 3) Make it measurable + visible

One **checkbox** per day.
Paper calendar.
Big X. (If it's not checkable, it's not real.)

### 4) Do a WOOP

**Wish:** Walk nightly.
**Outcome:** Better sleep + energy.
**Obstacle:** Tired after kids' bedtime.
**Plan: If** I feel wiped at 7, **then** I do **5 minutes** inside the house.

## 5) Set a stop rule

**If** I miss **2 days in a row**, **then** I must text one person from my Five and restart tonight within **2 minutes**.

No shame.
Just resume.

# Language Matters (identity > restriction)

**“I can’t skip tonight.”** → Argument with yourself.

**“I don’t skip—something is better than nothing.”** → Identity statement; debate closed.

(Research shows **“I don’t”** beats **“I can’t”** for sticking to commitments.)

# Micro-Examples

**Body:** *After dinner* I will walk 10 minutes. If it rains, then I march in place purposefully while I listen to an episode of the “Renovations of the Soul” podcast.

**Faith:** *When coffee brews* I will read one Psalm. If kids interrupt, I finish the reading with my kids.

**Work:** *At 9:00 a.m.* I will write 100 words. If I experience "writer's block", then I outline 3 bullets.

**Commitments you **can see** will forever be victorious over intentions you **can feel**.

**Try** makes you unstable.

**Do** makes you unshakable.

## Be a Quitter

This might sting: you need to learn to be a quitter.

"Don't be a quitter" has been a mantra poisoning the general population for decades. Coaches, parents, teachers—everyone hammered it in—quitting was weak.

It was shameful—I call bullshit.

A mentor of mine for a number of years smacked me in the face with this one day. For the record, his name is Martin Rooney, and he framed it like this: **"Be a quitter. Just learn to quit the right things."**

Quit what drains you.
Quit what chains you.
Quit what kills your spirit.
Quit what keeps you small.

Whatever holds you back from what you want most.
Quit it.

And Jesus told a parable that echoes this wholly—it tightens my stomach every time I read it.

## The Barren Fig Tree

Picture this:
A vineyard in full bloom. Vines heavy with grapes, workers wiping sweat from their brows.

Everything alive, everything producing, everything as expected, except one damn fig tree.

Tall, leafy, gorgeous—at a distance—but when the owner got up close, searching the branches, there's nothing.

Not one fig.
A fruitless tree just taking up space in the soil.

He grumbled while snapping a branch in frustration. You can hear the impatience in his voice.

"Three years," he mutters.
"Three years I've come looking for fruit on this thing. For nothing. Cut it down. Why should it waste the soil?"

The vineyard is prime real estate...every square foot of soil matters. Grapevines are thriving all around, pulling nutrients from the earth. And here's this fig tree, just standing there, leafy and proud, but contributing nothing.

A taker, not a giver.

Then, the gardener steps in. Tired eyes, but compassion in his voice. He put himself between the axe and the trunk.

"Sir, leave it alone for one more year," he pleads. "I'll dig around it. I'll spread manure. I'll do the dirty work. If it still doesn't bear fruit after that, fine. I'll cut it down."

That's heavy.
Because that tree is us.

We've all been the barren fig tree. Taking up space, looking alive on the outside, but producing jack shit on the inside.
And God, the owner of the vineyard, has every right to say, "Enough. Chop it down."

But Jesus, the Gardener, steps in.

He says, "Give them one more chance. I'll get my hands dirty. I'll do whatever it takes to wake them up, to bring fruit out of them."

That's grace.
That's patience.
But it's not forever.

If the fig tree still refuses to produce, eventually the axe must fall.

And that's where "fuck trying" hits hard. Because you don't get fruit from "trying." You don't get a bountiful—sustainable—harvest from half-ass efforts.

The fig tree had plenty of leaves, plenty of *appearance*, but no fruit. God is not impressed with appearances. He's looking for sweet and juicy fruit from what you ***do***.

***"Every branch in me that beareth not fruit he taketh away: and every branch that beareth fruit, he purgeth it, that it may bring forth more fruit."***
(John 15:2, KJV)

**So ask yourself:** are you a fig tree that's just standing there "trying," all leafy in appearance—but bears no fruit?
Or are you actually producing fruit—through your actions, your choices, your ***doing***?

Because one more season is a gift, not a guarantee.Don't waste it.

## Faith: Doing Versus Trying

Faith is the ultimate arena between doing and trying. It's so much more than being about your fitness goals or your career path. It's in everything.

Peter walking on water is the whole story in one scene: Jesus says, "Come." Then Peter steps out of the boat. And for a few glorious moments, he did the impossible.
Until he noticed what the wind was doing and shifted back into "try" mode—hesitation, doubt return—and he sinks (Matthew 14:29–31, KJV).

That's the heartbeat of faith: feet first, feelings later...maybe—if at all.

And the science rhymes with it harmoniously:
**Behavioral Activation** (depression treatment): shows how action precedes mood—not the other way around. People who schedule small, value-aligned actions (call the friend, take the walk, do the chore) see mood follow behavior, not "motivation" (Jacobson et al., late 1990s; Dimidjian et al., 2006).

**Translation:** you do, then you feel.

**Approach > Avoidance**: Decades of research on approach–avoidance conflict finds that when you step toward a valued goal, uncertainty and fear shrink; when you hover, they amplify.

**Translation:** Action reduces rumination. Rumination fuels doubt.

**Exposure & Inhibitory Learning**: Anxiety doesn't fade because you wait; it fades because you enter the feared situation, and stay long enough for your brain to learn "*I can survive this*" (Craske et al., 2014).

**Translation:** Faith feels the wind and steps out anyway—that's literally how fear gets rewired. **Don't wait until you feel ready. Move—then your brain catches up.**

Faith turns the headlights on and drives through the fog anyway.

# The Persistent Widow

Jesus told a story about a widow who didn't "try."
She persisted (Luke 18).

Imagine a dusty little village where everyone knows everybody's business.

There's a widow—poor, overlooked, and with no husband to defend her. And in those days, if you were a widow, you were basically invisible in society.

Now picture her walking, day after day, to the judge's courtyard.

This judge?

Crooked as hell—he did not fear God—neither did he give two shits about anyone else but himself.

The widow—No bribes, no power, no influence.

Just her voice.

And damn, did she use it.

"Give me justice against my adversary!" she cried.

The judge waved her off. But the next day...there she was again.

"Give me justice!"

Time passes.
He tries to outlast her.
But she just won't quit.

Finally, one day, he throws his hands up and mutters: "I don't give a damn about God, and I sure don't care about people. But this widow? She's driving me insane. If I don't give her justice, I will grow wearisome."

So he caves.
He rules in her favor.
Not because he suddenly grew a conscience, but because she did something over and over again until she succeeded.

For the fuck sake of Pete, stop whispering timid prayers and half-hearted promises.

Show up like the widow.
Knock until the door cracks open.

Or break it down.
You can absolutely wear life down with persistence.

## The Energy Drain

The cost of trying: it can bleed you dry.

Every "I'll try" is a half-open tab in your brain.

Like having 37 apps running in the background on your phone, sucking the battery, and slowing the entire system down.

You wonder why you're tired, anxious, burned out? Check how many of your "tries" are draining your soul.

Trying is indecision stretched out over weeks, months, maybe even years.

Doing is decisive.

It costs energy upfront, but then it clears the bandwidth—conserving energy in the long run.

# Field Work: Close the Back Door

**Purpose:** Turn "I'll try" into "I do." No loopholes. No half-measures.

**Time:** 18 minutes

**Tools:** Pen + paper (or Notes app), calendar, and one small target

### Step 1 — Catch the "Try"

Write the sentence you've been saying:

"I'll try to ______."

Now slash it.
Replace it with one of these (binary, like Jesus said):

"I **will** ______."
"I **won't** ______."

### Step 2 — Name the Seed

Pick **one** concrete aim for the next 6 weeks (small enough to repeat):

**Examples:**
"10-minute walk"

"One Psalm"

"100 words"

"Marriage check-in"

"Protein first at lunch"

Write it out:
**"My seed is: ______."**

## Step 3 — Set the Trigger (If–Then)

This is where you shut the back door.Fill this in:

**IF** it is ______ (time/event), **THEN** I will ______ (exact action) for ______ minutes.

**Examples:**
If coffee brews, then I read one Psalm.

If dishes are done, then I walk 10 minutes.

If it's 9:00 a.m., then I write 100 words.

## Step 4 — Make it Visible

Create a simple proof system:

Draw **42 boxes** (6 weeks)

Label it: **DO > TRY**

Every day you do the rep, you check a box.

If it's not checkable, it's not real.

## Step 5 — 60 Second WOOP

Do this fast. No essays.

**Wish:** ______

**Outcome:** ______

**Obstacle:** ______

**Plan:** If ______ happens, then I will ______ anyway.

## Step 6 — Stop Rule

Set the rule **now**, not after you fail.

**If I miss 2 days in a row, then ______.**

Examples:

text one person from my Five

restart tonight with 2 minutes

move the trigger earlier tomorrow

**No shame.**
**Just restart immediately.**

## Receipts:

Do **one** of these right now:

Screenshot your calendar reminder for the trigger, **or**

Text someone: “I’m done ‘trying.’ Ask me tomorrow if I checked my box.”

## Ask yourself:

Where am I keeping one foot on the dock?

# Wrapping Up

Yoda knew it.
Aesop knew it.
Jesus knew it.

The tortoise won because he **did**.
The son who worked the vineyard pleased his father because he **did**.
The widow got justice because she **did**.

“I’ll try” is a stall tactic.
A limp handshake with life.

Doing is the only way forward.

So fuck trying.

Quit the dead weight.
Burn the ships.
Put on the seatbelt.
Rotate the tires.

And for the fuck sake of Pete, stop hedging your bets.

Do. Learn. Do it again.
That’s the only way you will grow.

And the sooner you stop “trying” and start “doing,” the sooner you'll start accomplishing more cool shit.

Because you stop throwing stumblingblocks ahead of your path.

But let's get one thing straight—**doing doesn't mean doing it perfectly.**

Doing means you **show up honest.**
You take the rep.
You get feedback.
You adjust.
You return.

Trying loves the idea of "someday."
Doing lives for **today**—even if today is small.

"Trying" keeps one foot on the dock while the boat's already drifting away.

"Trying" is fear in disguise...dressed up as honest effort, yet dripping with doubt and hesitation.

It sounds noble, but it's really the **ego** hedging **your** bets.

Because if you "try" and fail, you can always say, "Well, at least I tried."

But "do"?

Do leaves no back door.
Do is commitment in motion.
Do demands faithfulness.

It's Peter stepping out of the boat before he knew if he could walk on water.

## FVCK IT

It’s David running toward Goliath with a slingshot and a heartbeat full of faith.

It’s Jesus saying, “Follow Me,” and the disciples dropping everything...no Plan B, no safety net, no “try.”

I'll say it again—because I like this one—fuck trying.

Stop standing at the edge of your own calling.
Pick up the pen.
Send the message.
Start the damn thing.

Not when you feel ready.
Not when the wind dies down.

**Now.**

Because “trying” is built on doubt.
Doing is built on faith.

God doesn’t bless your intentions.
He blesses your actions.

He does't care about how good you look.
He cares about what good you do.

***“Faith without works is dead”*** (James 2:17, KJV)

So maybe the miracle you’re waiting for isn’t to wait on God at all.

Maybe He is waiting for you to move.

Trying keeps you safe.
Doing makes you dangerous.

It's the moment hesitation dies and obedience is born.

The moment you stop bargaining with your potential and start becoming who the hell you were made to be.

Because the Kingdom doesn't come through effort.
It comes through execution of good works through your soul.

**And once you start executing, don't be surprised when the next enemy shows up wearing a church suit and carrying a stopwatch.**

# Chapter 6

# Fvck Expectations

**Ego Alert:** Expectations can turn into a calendar invite to resentment.

**Vow:** I drop the script. I communicate. I choose peace over control.

# Highly Disappointed

**“Expectations are nothing more than premeditated disappointments.”**

I have no clue who said that but it was genius—and probably exhausted from them.

Because expectations are everywhere.
Not just for other people—for you, too.

I stacked them like cherries on top of a stressed out sundae: internal expectations, other people’s expectations (spouses, bosses, friends, neighbors), then the big umbrellas—culture, government, society, and the algorithmic gods listening through your phone.

At times I would wonder how it all started.

Then I remember: God.

He set the first expectation—But many of us have lost sight of what matters most.

We lost our way with the script and forgot the plot. Worse, we forget (or ignore, or get proud and stubborn) that different cultures carry different social expectations too.

So we walk around offended all day...because we’re playing different games and assuming everyone else read our custom rulebook.

Before we dive into the guts of this hearty chapter—we need to first gain a perspective of the sheer volume we juggle daily. These are only the expectations I could think of...I'd say it's time to get a grip on them.

## The Big Buckets

**Self:** who you "should" be by now—productivity, appearance, emotional control, success, timelines, status.

**Family:** loyalty, caregiving, holidays, traditions, elder care, values, careers, interests.

**Friendships:** availability, reciprocity, confidentiality, crisis response time.

**Work & Money:** performance, promotions, milestones, hustle norms, after-hours access.

**Health & Body:** baseline, diet, fitness, sobriety, beauty standards, "aging well."

**Romance, Intimacy, & Sex:** frequency, depth, initiation, what "support" means, exclusivity rules, kinks, fetishes.

**Time & Communication:** reply speeds, punctuality, planners vs. spontaneity, check-in cadence.

**Home & Domestic:** cleanliness, mental load, chore fairness, parenting styles.

**Community & Culture:** etiquette, politics, codes of dress/speech, neighborhood duties.

**Education & Growth:** degrees, skills, "figure it out" speed, endless upskilling.

**Spirituality & Meaning:** beliefs, practices, giving, moral narratives.

**Digital Life:** posting cadence, privacy, texting tone, read receipts, location sharing, rituals.

**Life Stages:** the "by-when"s—move out, marry, kids, house, retirement, legacy.

And yeah—there's more—a lot more.
But we need to move the fuck on.

**Pause & Breathe.**
Inhale white clouds, exhale grey clouds.
Then ask yourself:

How often am I disappointed because someone didn't meet my expectations?

Is this disappointment worth the expectation?

Which expectations am I willing to let go of?

What expectations of myself are quietly poisoning my joy?

Now that you're in your feels—#sorrynotsorry—let's talk about how expectations work in the brain.

More specifically, how they can short-circuit your brain.

## Your Brain on Dru...
## I Mean Expectations

Here's the nerd edition that explains the rage, the letdown, and the looping resentment—and how to break it.

Remember, your brain is a prediction engine.
It constantly guesses what comes next so it can conserve energy.

**Expectations are filters attempting to make the guessing game easier.**

When reality clashes with your script, you feel a sharp "prediction error"—that neural pinch you feel in your nervous system. **Reward prediction error research** explains why "better than expected" feels like a hit and "worse than expected" feels like a crash (Schultz and follow-ups).

**Translation:** disappointment is not random. It's a mathematical calculation error between your map and reality.

**A few more traps:**

**Affective forecasting errors:** we're bad at predicting what will make us happy—and for how long (Gilbert & Wilson). So we overbuild expectations and under-deliver reality, then blame life for not matching a fantasy we invented.

**Hedonic adaptation:** you adapt fast; the bar moves; expectations climb.
That thrill you had yesterday becomes "meh" today (Brickman & Campbell).

**Confirmation bias + relationship lenses:** your unspoken rules become filters—your brain sees what confirms them and misses what contradicts them.

**Cultural scripts:** what counts as "respectful," "on time," or "supportive" varies from person to person. Treating your script as universal is the fastest way to be offended all day.

***"Hope deferred maketh the heart sick: but when the desire cometh, it is a tree of life."***
(Proverbs 13:12, KJV)

Expectation without clarity becomes deferred hope—and it hardens your heart. Bearing fruit of darkness like resentment, hate, bitterness, and judgement.

Expectations are a contract you hand someone—but there's no time to review the document together, collect signatures, and have it notarized.

Then punish them for "breaking contract."
That's not mature.
That's psychic debt collection.

**Good news:** expectations aren't evil—they're just unchecked predictions.

The fix isn't to feel nothing—check it out:

**Replace expectations with agreements.**
Agreements must be spoken to be agreed on.
Names. Terms. Negotiated. Owned. Clear.

Expectations are silent.
Romantic.
Unrealistic.
Bitter-builders.

If less disappointment is what you want—more expectations is not the answer.

Don't become colder.
Become more clear.

Clarity isn't mean.
Clarity is love without confusion.

# The Fix

## Turn Expectations into Agreements & Outcomes into Standards

**Expectation (unstated)**: *"You should know what I need."*→
**Agreement (stated)**: *"Here's what I need; can we agree to X?"*

**Expectation (outcome)**: *"We must hit this exact result."*→ **Standard (process)**: *"We show up at 6 a.m., three days a week—no negotiations."*

**Expectation (mind-reading)**: *"Text me back fast, or you don't care."*→ **Agreement (clarity)**: *"Can we agree to a 24-hour reply window unless it's urgent?"*

***"He hath shewed thee, O man, what is good; and what doth the LORD require of thee, but to do justly, and to love mercy, and to walk humbly with thy God?"*** (Micah 6:8, KJV)

God's expectations are clear and few...I mean they are now, thanks be to Jesus.

But we're the ones turning life into a bunch of fine print.

## When Expectations Belong to God (not you)

Some expectations are above your pay grade: timing, outcomes, how other people respond.

Your job is obedience.
God's job is the outcome.

This is plastered throughout the Bible:

*"My soul, wait thou only upon God; for my expectation is from him."* (Psalm 62:5, KJV)

*"Take therefore no thought for the morrow: for the morrow shall take thought for the things of itself. Sufficient unto the day is the evil thereof."* (Matthew 6:34, ESV).

**Swap it:**

**Outcome**: "This must happen by June."

**Obedience**: "I'll do today's faithful step; God owns the clock."

Anger spikes when **reality ≠ expectation**.
Sometimes that anger is holy (injustice).

Often it's from a contract no one signed.

**Two moves:**

1. **Make it an agreement** (ask, don't assume).

2. **Make it a standard** (a process you control, not an outcome you don't).

## The Ugly, The Bad, and The Fucking Fantastic

I was going to call this section *"The Good, The Bad, and The Ugly."* It rolls off the tongue better.

But let's be honest—life isn't always cinematic. Sometimes it's just you eating some overcooked noodles...

...while everyone stares at each other to figure out who the villain is because no one helped.

So—we'll start with the ugliest of expectations first. Why not drag you through the trenches before laying on the beach?

## The Ugly (Corrosive Expectations)

There are absolutely bullshit expectations: misplaced, unrealistic, and sometimes completely destructive.

**Cultural Timelines:** Society tells you that by 30 you should have the house, the car, the partner, the savings account, and the six-pack abs.

Reality check?

The average American household carries over $100,000 in debt, and only 39% of adults report feeling financially secure (Federal Reserve, 2023). Yet the pressure persists, and when you don't "measure up," shame takes the wheel.

**Inherited Expectations:** These are the ones whispered—or screamed—at you from childhood. Maybe it was "Don't disappoint the family," or "Real men don't cry," or "If you're not the top student, you're nothing."

Psychologists call this **internalized parental expectations**, and research shows they're directly correlated with perfectionism, anxiety, and depression later in life (Flett & Hewitt, 2014).

**Self-Inflicted:** Sometimes the ugliest battlefield is the one in your own head. You set impossible standards, raise the bar higher every time you barely clear it, and punish yourself relentlessly for not being superhuman.

Neuroscience shows this creates a toxic loop. The dopamine reward systems get hijacked by failure, leading to chronic dissatisfaction and burnout (Bress et al., 2017).

The result?

A brain wired to anticipate failure more than success.
A psyche that confuses self-worth with constant achievement.
A soul that feels like it's on trial facing the death penalty every damn day.

And here's the kicker: these ugly expectations aren't just harmless illusions.

They're **stressors that negatively impact the body**.

Chronic exposure to unmet or unrealistic expectations spikes cortisol, rewires the amygdala, and makes you more vulnerable to cardiovascular disease, weakened immunity, and major depressive episodes (McEwen, 2007).

**In other words:** this isn't just "in your head." It's in every fucking one of your body's ~30 trillion cells.

## The Bad (Noble... Until It Eats You)

If *The Ugly* are the ones we need to irradicate, *The Bad* start out looking noble but end up chewing you alive.

**The "Almost" Expectations:** These are the expectations we set that are achievable in theory but destructive in practice.

"I should always be available for my friends."
"I should hold onto my feelings until the time is right."
"I should never lose my temper."
"I should give 110% at work, even if it kills me."

These aren't outright lies, but they leave zero margin for error. Psychologists call this **maladaptive perfectionism**, and it's strongly tied to higher anxiety, procrastination, and reduced resilience (Shafran et al., 2002).

**The Moving Goalpost Effect:** You hit the milestone—promotion, degree, follower count—and before the champagne is flat, you've already told yourself it's not enough. Your brain adapts frighteningly fast: the dopamine surge you get from success fades quickly, leading to **hedonic adaptation** (Brickman & Campbell, 1971).

**Translation:** the "high" wears off, and you're left chasing the next fix.

**Conditional Joy:** "I'll be happy when I…"
This little phrase is a poison pill. It ties your joy to some external checkbox, leaving your psyche on permanent layaway.

Studies show people who base their self-worth on external performance are far more likely to experience depression, poor sleep, and chronic stress (Crocker & Wolfe, 2001).

The Bad isn't as obvious as The Ugly. It sneaks in under the radar, dressed up as ambition, discipline, honor, and loyalty.

But over time, it slowly hollows you out.

***"Hope deferred maketh the heart sick: but when the desire cometh, it is a tree of life."***
(Proverbs 13:12, KJV)

When you keep deferring hope, when fulfillment is always tied to the next expectation, you're not living.

You're bargaining with your own soul.

## The Fucking Fantastic (The Ones Worth Keeping)

Now here's the twist: not all expectations are toxic. Some are rocket fuel. Some are the scaffolding that holds your best self together.

**Stretch Expectations:** These are the ones that push you past your comfort zone without breaking you. They activate the brain's **zone of proximal development**—a sweet spot where challenge meets capability (Vygotsky, 1978).

These expectations build grit, confidence, and long-term mastery.

**Shared Expectations:** When expectations are grounded in community. Be it family, friendships, faith, they foster accountability and connection. Research on **social baseline theory** shows that when we face challenges alongside others, our brains literally use fewer resources; stress diminishes, and we endure longer (Beckes & Coan, 2011).

**Simply put:** expectations borne together don't weigh as much.

**Hopeful Expectations:** This is where psychology and spirituality shake hands. Optimistic expectations. What psychologists call **positive expectancy**; are linked to better health, stronger immune function, and longer life spans (Carver & Scheier, 2014).

Spiritually, this is faith in action.

***"Now faith is the substance of things hoped for, the evidence of things not seen."*** (Hebrews 11:1, KJV)

When your expectations align with hope and faith, they don't crush you.

They carry you.

The Fucking Fantastic expectations are the ones that remind you of who you are—and who you're becoming.

They don't drag you into a pit of shame.
They don't keep you chained to the moving goalpost.

They say: *Stretch. Bend. Sway. Reach. Risk. Trust.*

And when you meet or exceed them, the brain rewards you with joy, resilience, and even deeper trust in the ***process***.

This is where the trenches give way to the beach.
Where the weight lifts.
Where the grind turns into glory.

But even if you clean up the 'good' and 'bad' expectations, there's a whole category that keeps wrecking lives from the shadows.

# Bonus Round: The Never Expectations

**The Ninjas (Ghost Rules/Mafia Clauses)**
These are the invisible contracts you never articulate... but you punish people for breaking them. I'm not saying it's out of malicious intent—but it happens all too often.

These are the **Ghost Rules** of relationships and life.

The assumptions we never articulate but still punish people for breaking.

They pop up **in marriages**
("You should've *known* I needed help"),
**in friendships**
("If you cared, you'd have just shown up"),
and **in workplaces**
("If they valued me, they'd already be paying me more").

It's like everyone else is supposed to have a copy of the script, but you're the only one who's actually read it.

Social psychologists call this **psychological contract breach**. Basically, the **Mafia Clause** of expectations: "It was understood." (Spoiler: it wasn't.)
When these hidden deals get "violated," trust collapses, even though the other side never agreed in the first place (Rousseau, 1995).

Neuroscience shows that unmet social expectations—especially the sneaky, silent kind—light up the same circuits as physical pain (Eisenberger & Lieberman, 2004).

That's why being let down by someone who "should've known better" hits harder than stubbing your pinky toe on the coffee table.

Relationship experts call this the **Trap Door Effect**. Everything looks fine on the surface until one wrong step sends the whole thing crashing down (Gottman & Silver, 1999).

**The way out:** drag it into the light.

**Say It Out Loud:** Unless you're married to a psychic, they can't read your mind.

**Check Assumptions:** Instead of "they should know," ask yourself, "Did I ever actually tell them?"

**Negotiate Reality:** Expectations turn into agreements only when both sides consciously sign off.

***"Ye lust, and have not: ye kill, and desire to have, and cannot obtain: ye fight and war, yet ye have not, because ye ask not."*** (James 4:2, KJV)

If God Himself requires you to voice your needs—the people at your table deserve the same courtesy. Jesus even told this to us in multiple places—but my favorite is the Gospel According to John:

***"Whatever you ask in my name, this I will do, that the Father may be glorified in the Son. If you ask me anything in my name, I will do it."***
(John 14:13-14, KJV)

The **Ninjas**, **Ghost Rules**, and **Mafia Clauses** of life aren't just misunderstandings. They breed bitterness and unsolicited resentment if they are left unchecked.

Once they're said aloud; they transform into opportunities for clarity, connection, and—dare I say—some comedy.

## To Suffer or Flow

When life happens and shit doesn't work out how *you expected*—Ope! No pun intended—that's when the spiraling can begin.

When plans crumble, you feel like everyone around you is disappointed, maybe you're disappointed in yourself.

Shit hurts and it can feel real fucking heavy.
It may even feel like everyone is against you, even God.

Anger boils.
Resentment builds.

Your frustrations spew over into your home—onto your loved ones—or even strangers.

Your family doesn't deserve it.
You don't deserve it.

And the little old lady just trying to get her husband to chemo sure as hell didn't deserve your middle finger because she was "driving too slow."

Pause.
Breathe.

Remember this: **everyone has their own unique story.**

Everyone is carrying their own pile of shit; and they really are doing their best to keep it in one pile.

How about we stop going around tossing handfuls of our own shit on other people's pile?

Maybe that little old lady is scared to death of all the reckless drivers on the road.
Her husband isn't allowed to drive because of the chemo and she is all he has.

She still prays to Jesus that the person who flipped her off gets to where they need to be on time.

At times, I feel people expect so much from everyone else in the world that they've lost sight of what their own inner child has *always* expected from them.

Few live up to these childhood "expectations."

*(Pssst...they're your fucking passions. And despite age, no passion is too childish. They're your compass to freedom, peace, and happiness.)*

The "I want to be an astronaut when I grow up," passions.

Well, why aren't you an astronaut?

(*Or whatever the fuck it was for you.)*

## Martha & Mary (Expectations vs Presence)

Jesus entered a small village and Martha welcomed *Him* into her home. Immediately, she kicked into host mode.
Dishes clattering, bread baking, water hauling.
Sweat on her brow, dust on her hands.

She was consumed with *expectations*. The role of the woman. The hostess. The one who had to hold everything together.

Meanwhile, her sister Mary was acting all scandalous and shit.

She sat at Jesus' feet.
Not in the kitchen.
Not in the background.

She sat in the place of a disciple, wide-eyed, soaking in every word He spoke to them.

Martha snapped, she had a tantrum in front of everyone. She stormed up to Jesus, anger laced with exhaustion. "Lord, don't you care that my sister has left me to do the work alone? Tell her to help me!"

But Jesus didn't side with her. He looked at her with tenderness and said,

***"Martha, Martha, thou art careful and troubled about many things: But one thing is needful: and Mary hath chosen that good part, which shall not be taken away from her."*** (Luke 10:41-42, KJV)

Do you see it?

Martha was buried under the weight of expectation...society's, culture's, her own.

She thought her worth was in performance.
She thought her value was in juggling all the things.

Mary broke the script.

She refused to be measured by what was expected.

She sat down.
She listened.

She chose presence over pressure.

Expectations will chain you to performance.
Presence will free you.

The world says, "Do more."
Jesus says, "Choose better."

## The Energy Cost of Suffering

Here's the paradox: suffering actually takes **more energy** than flowing with life.

**Psychology suggests:** Resisting your emotions, what researchers call ***experiential avoidance***, is exhausting. Suppressing anger, fear, or sadness activates your brain's stress circuits in overdrive, leaving you depleted (Gross & Levenson, 1997; Hayes et al., 1996). Chronic stress keeps your cortisol high, which burns out your body's systems (McEwen, 2007).

**Neuroscience proved it:** Flow states are the opposite. When you stop fighting and lean into presence, your brain actually becomes more efficient. You use less energy to do more. Time feels lighter. Effort feels easier (Csikszentmihalyi, 1990; Dietrich, 2004).

Jesus said it clear as day:

***"For my yoke is easy and my burden is light."***
(Matthew 11:30, KJV)

Flow with Him, and the weight lifts.

***"For thus the Lord God, the Holy One of Israel; In returning and rest shall ye be saved; in quietness and in confidence shall be your strength: and ye would not."*** (Isaiah 30:15, KJV)

Strength doesn't come from striving, it comes from surrender.

## What Are We Supposed to Surrender?

We're not asked to surrender our passion—our dreams—or our grit.

Those ***are*** the gifts.
Those are the bread and the butter.

Those are the things you're ***not*** supposed to surrender.

**Things to Surrender:** This isn't an exhaustive list of course. Do some research.

**The Illusion of Control** – That constant need to force outcomes, micromanage people, and wrestle life into your version of "how it should be."
Psychology shows this is a losing battle: when we cling to control, our stress skyrockets, but when we practice acceptance and surrender this false sense of control, our anxiety drops and resilience rises (Hayes et al., 1996).

**The Need to Strive for Worth** – The grind that says "I'll be enough when..." Scripture flips that lie on its head. **Ephesians 2:8-9** reminds us we are saved by grace, not by performance. Flow happens when you stop hustling for your worth and start living from your worth.

**The Bitterness of Unforgiveness** – Resentment is heavy. Forgiveness isn't excusing what happened. It's setting down a weight you were never meant to drag for miles. **Hebrews 12:15** warns that bitterness takes root and poisons everything.

Surrender it, and space opens for healing.

**The Fear of Failing** – Fear is energy-draining. Neuroscience shows fear keeps your amygdala hyperactive, hijacking focus and motivation (LeDoux, 2000).

When you surrender fear—whether of rejection, failure, or loss—you get back energy to actually create, love, and move forward.

Surrender isn't weakness.
It's wisdom.

## The Crossroads

This is where the fork in the road appears.

**You have two options:**

**Option 1: Suffer.**

Keep resisting what is. Keep blaming others. Keep clenching so hard against reality that your spirit bruises under the pressure.

Neuroscience backs this up: when you resist emotional pain, your brain's stress circuits amplify it, creating a vicious cycle (Hayes et al., 1996).

Suffering isn't just about the pain—it's the meaning you attach to the pain.

**Option 2: Flow.**

Release the death-grip on how it *should have been and how it should be,* then let life carry you like a river.

Flow doesn't erase pain; it lets you ride through it without having to struggle at keeping your head above water.

It's not a resignation.
It's wisdom.

It's strength.

It's surrender.

## What Flow Looks Like

Flow doesn't mean life gets easy. It means you stop fighting the river. It looks like:

Choosing response over reaction.

Looking at a setback and asking, "What's this here to teach me?"

Returning to your inner child's curiosity instead of your adult ego's anger.

Releasing the myth of control, and practicing faith instead of fear.

***"Trust in the LORD with all thine heart; and lean not unto thine own understanding. In all thy ways acknowledge him, and he shall direct thy paths."***
(Proverbs 3:5-6, KJV)

Flow is trust in action. It's throwing paint at a canvas and trusting an image to emerge.

Suffering is to swim upstream until your muscles give out

Flow is chilling in a tube just float'n around; enjoying the ride.

Both take you somewhere, but only one leaves you with energy for the rest of the journey ahead.

## Your Choice

So I'll ask you again: do you want to continue to suffer?

Or do you want to flow along with life like a river tube ride—arms stretched wide, sun on your face—laughing with the rapids instead of cursing at them?

The choice won't erase your pain. But it will change your relationship with it.
And sometimes, that shift makes all the difference between drowning in resentment and floating freely.

It could just be what saves your relationships.

## The Dopamine of Unexpected Respect

Here's a twist you might not *expect*: I've found it's actually better to sometimes **expect disrespect**.

(Da fuck?! Why?) Yeah...I know right. But listen...

Because when respect does show up, it hits harder.

Remember **positive prediction error**? When reality turns out better than you anticipated, your brain's reward system throws a dopamine party (Schultz, 2016). Respect feels sweeter because it wasn't assumed.

Nancy Cantor and Julie Norem studied this under the label ***defensive pessimism*** (Norem & Cantor, 1986).

By lowering expectations—people were able to manage their anxiety and set themselves up for the pleasant surprise of success. The same logic applies here: if you brace for coldness but receive kindness, the warmth feels extraordinary.

But here's the warning label: live this way long-term and it can curdle into cynicism. If you always expect disrespect, you'll stop giving people the chance to surprise you. Relationships can't thrive in a garden of distrust.

Scripture offers a sharper balance: don't anchor your worth to whether others honor or dishonor you at all.

***"Be kindly affectioned one to another with brotherly love; in honour preferring one another;"*** (Romans 12:10 KJV)

***"For they loved the praise of men more than the praise of God."*** (John 12:43, KJV)

That verse is a warning label against human validation—it's addictive, and rots the soul quietly.

So yes, expecting disrespect can give you a dopamine bump when respect does happen to show up.

But the real power is this:

When your value isn't chained to human opinion ("Fvck What They Think"), every act of respect becomes icing on the cake.

Without ever letting it become ***the*** whole cake.

Don't let someone else mix, make, and bake your cake.

I look for my worth from God and that's only because I already looked everywhere else.

## Circling Back

Unspoken expectations are the most dangerous.

We covered that—but I really want to stress the importance of this. Because I have found some things in life just need repetition and this seems to be one of them in my past relationships.

To be honest—we all benefit from eliminating the unspoken ones completely.

If you and your partner sit down and set agreements out together. Fucking fantastic!

But tread carefully...

It's important to be absolutely, crystal, fucking, clear.

Write them down. When it's on paper, it's harder to argue—and it's easier to agree.

Make them stupidly obvious.
Realistic and clear expectations are a serious matter.

John the Baptist is a perfect example of how expectations can work against us.

As John's expectation was based on prophecy; it was filtered through human interpretation. He saw judgment and assumed it meant conquest. He saw "the kingdom" and assumed it meant political power.

But Jesus came to wage a deeper war, not against Rome, but against sin, death, and the powers of darkness.

John was looking for a lion; Jesus came as a lamb.

John even questioned Jesus as the Messiah and Jesus responded gracefully (Matthew 11:4-6, KJV) with a list of reminders to John of Jesus' good works.

**Translation:** John, I am the Messiah—just not the kind you expected.

And so...

What's realistic?
What's not?

That's for you to discern.
Yup, more decisions.

But these decisions are a demand—an action toward alignment—and that hit of dopamine.

**The punchline:**
Three frogs sit on the bank of a river.
Two decide to jump in.

How many frogs are left sitting on the riverbank?

Three.

A decision is only a thought until action makes it happen.

## The Common Failures

The most common failure I see with expectations, whether with yourself or with others, is lack of follow-through.

Accountability fucking matters.

If an expectation is set but never reinforced, is it really an expectation?

And just getting angry about it, yelling your piece and moving on, isn't really accountability.
That's only a reaction. A piss poor one at that.

I've watched people set expectations, then ignore them being unmet, and then get angry later when all the other shit hits the fan.

Often, it's unconscious.
Very rarely is it with malicious intent.
That doesn't diminish the damage it can cause.

It usually starts with a “small” thing: *Take the garbage out every Wednesday night.*

No big deal, right?
Then one week it doesn’t happen.

No consequence.
No word.
Just silence.

Then again...
And again...
Next thing you know, the little cracks turn to fractures and fractures to fault lines.

Unmet micro-expectations can erode trust faster than big betrayals—because they accumulate invisibly over time until there's a breaking point (Rousseau, 1995; Gottman & Silver, 1999).

Also—on a serious note—can we let go of holding onto shit?

Sayyyy something.
Then—drop it in the Fires of Yesterday.

Rumination keeps your stress hormones jacked like the gym bruh dry scooping pre-workout between sets (Brosschot et al., 2006).

Forgiveness though?
Forgiveness lowers blood pressure and strengthens your body’s defenses (Worthington & Scherer, 2004).

***"Remember ye not the former things, neither consider the things of old"*** (Isaiah 43:18, KJV)

Plainly said, don't dwell on the past—you need to forget about it.

## Demons of the Past and the Future

There are two demons that feed on your time.
I named mine **Remorael** and **Vexra**.

Remorael is the Demon of the Past—the Clinger. He wraps around my memories and whispers:
*"You should've known better."*
*"You could've done more."*
*"You would've been enough if..."*

And science now confirms what the soul has always felt: replaying our regrets can re-ignite the same neural circuits as the original pain.
A Mount Sinai study (2022) found that the brain processes two distinct types of regret in separate regions. Each one is linked to stress and mood disorders.

So when Remorael whispers, he's not a myth.
He's the chemical echo of the past hijacking your peace.
He's measurable. He's real.

Then comes **Vexra**, the Demon of the Future—The Tempter of "Someday."

Her voice drips with promise and panic:
*"You should be there by now."*
*"You could've made it if you just tried harder."*
*"You would be happy if life finally went your way."*

Studies show the mind's ***anticipation of regret*** is one of the strongest emotional drivers of behavior (Abraham & Sheeran, 2016).
That "fear of future disappointment" fires the same stress pathways as physical threat. And when you live in that state long enough, your brain wires itself for anxiety.

A recent study found that pessimistic future expectations—believing *I'll never be enough*—are directly tied to depression and loss of agency (O'Sullivan et al., 2023).

Remorael and Vexra are siblings.
Born of the same evil parent.

Remorael tells you to rewrite the past.
Vexra tells you to micromanage the future.

Both demons whisper in the language of *Should. Could. Would.*
But the voice of God doesn't speak in *should, could,* or *would.*

He speaks in ***"I AM."*** (Exodus 3:14, KJV)

The eternal present.
The holy now.

So yes; **"Fuck expectations"** isn't rebellion.

It's recovery. It's neuroscience and soul care colliding.
Every expectation—even the ones you put on yourself.

## Self-Expectations

Expectations on yourself can be powerful tools—or brutal traps.

It depends on how you frame them.

Just like with others, your expectations must come with consequences. Otherwise they're just fucking hopes and dreams—like people who tell me all the cool shit they'd do if they won the Powerball, but never buy a ticket.

So—this is tricky. Real fucking tricky.
Because the relationship with yourself is the most important one you'll ever have.

Set expectations without compassion, and you can drown in guilt and self-hatred.
Set them with clarity and kindness, and they become the rails that keep your life on track.

Self-compassion actually strengthens follow-through more than self-criticism (Neff, 2003).

If you have unmet expectations with yourself, you can't just divorce yourself like you can with another person. You're stuck together—and so when you fail your own expectations (like how I didn't meet a single self-appointed deadline for this book) it hurts in a unique way.

Sure, sometimes you'll meet or exceed them.
But most of us fall short here and there.
Especially with those we hold close.

## Expectations in Relationships

Expectations can easily put unnecessary strain on relationships—often a breeding ground for guilt, manipulation, and resentment—when the expectations are not clear, agreed upon, and lived.

I hold firm expectations for my kids—becuase they need structure to become decent humans:

**Approaching situations with love and kindness**

**Wash hands and face after a meal**

**Take care of your body (brush your damn teeth)**

**Take care of your mind**

**Leave an area how you found it or better**

**Follow your passions—don't settle for less**

My dad used to ground me "for a month"... then lift it after a few days.

You know what I learned?

That his word meant nothing. So my behavior only got worse cause I mean *"what else can I get away with?"*

Expectations without follow-through are useless.
They can create rebellion, distrust, and more chaos.

***"Better is it that thou shouldest not vow, that that thou shouldest vow and not pay."***
(Ecclesiastes 5:5, KJV)

Words without follow-through erode trust faster than silence.

And yeah—I still struggle here too.

I over-book myself.

I say yes but forget timelines.

I say I'll do something but leave out when I'll do it—and if you don't give me a deadline—I'll assume it's fine on my timeline.

## So...What Now?

Let me be real clear with this.

Expectations aren't evil.

They just need clarity, realistic consequences, and self-awareness.

I've learned to lower the bar for others—much, much lower.
Because I can't control anyone but me.
I can only control my responses to others.

For example...instead of saying:
*"I expect my partner not to cheat on me."*

I say:
*"I will not tolerate unfaithfulness. If it happens, I will remove myself from the relationship."*

See the difference?

I'm not controlling them.
I'm controlling myself.

The expectation—a healthy and clear one—is on me, not them.

This is what psychologists call **internal locus of control** (Rotter, 1966).

By placing responsibility on your own choices rather than outsourcing power to others—you find yourself happier, healthier, and more resilient.

Imagine that—you're less stressed when you let people be them and you take care of you being yourself.

# Field Work:
# The Expectation Conversion Sprint

**Goal:**
In one week, you will:

**Expose** your top 3 expectations (including one "ninja")

**Convert** them into: **Agreement + Boundary + Standard**

**Ship** one real conversation/message

**Reduce** daily disappointment by lowering ghost rules and raising clarity.

**What you need:**
10 minutes/day

Notes app or paper

One "candle" person (trusted friend) *optional but powerful*

## Day 1 — The Inventory (Find the landmines)

Write **12 expectations** you've been carrying lately:
**4 about someone else.**
**4 about yourself.**
**4 about life/God/society.**

No poetry. Just the truth.

"I expect ____ to ____."

"People should ____."

"I should be ____ by now."

"If they cared, they would ____."

"I shouldn't have to ask for ____." (usually a ninja)

**Now circle your Top 3**:

One about someone else

One about yourself

One about life/God/timing

## Day 2 — The Ninja Hunt (Expose the ghost rule)

Pick the one that creates the most resentment.

Write it like a contract:

**Ninja Expectation:** "They should've known ____ without me saying it."

Now answer:

Did I ever say this out loud? **Yes / No**
Did we ever agree to it? **Yes / No**
Am I punishing them anyway? **Yes / No**

If you answered **"No / No / Yes"** — congratulations, you've been charging late fees on a contract nobody signed.

**Upgrade it** (1 sentence):

"I've been expecting ___ without saying it. I want to be clear: can we agree to ___?"

## Day 3 — Convert: Agreement / Boundary / Standard

Take your Top 3 and convert each one.

### 1) Expectation → Agreement (spoken, mutual)

**Expectation:** ______________________
**Agreement Request:** "Can we agree to
____________________ ?"
**Check:** specific? measurable? realistic? (Yes/No)

### 2) Expectation → Boundary (your action, your control)

**Expectation:** ______________________
**Boundary:** "If ______________, then I will
__________________."
**Example:** "If disrespect starts, then I end the conversation."

### 3) Expectation → Standard (process you control)

**Expectation:** ______________________
**Standard:** "I do __________________ on __________________."
**Example:** "I check my bank app every Monday/Thursday."

**Checklist:**

1 Agreement drafted: **Yes/No**

1 Boundary drafted: **Yes/No**

1 Standard drafted: **Yes/No**

## Day 4 — Ship the Message (No more imaginary conversations)

Send **one** real message today. Keep it clean.

### Text script (copy/paste)

"Hey—quick clarity check. I realized I've been expecting **[X]** without actually saying it. That's on me. Can we agree to **[Y]** going forward?"

If it's emotional or complex, you can **add**:

"I'm not mad. I'm trying to reduce resentment and be clear."

**Non-negotiable:** you send it today.

Not "I'll try."
You send it.

## Day 5 — The Crossroads Choice (Suffer or Flow)

This day is about **your relationship with reality**, not controlling anyone else.

Pick one situation you're currently resisting (work, family, money, relationship).

Then write:

**What I wanted:**

**What is happening:**

**The story I'm telling about it:**

**What I can control (3 things):**

**1**

**2**

**3**

**My "Flow Move" (one action today):**

**Rule:** Flow isn't passive.

Flow is **choosing the next faithful step without the chokehold.**

## Day 6 — The Dopamine Flip (Unexpected Respect, without becoming cynical)

This is NOT "expect disrespect forever."
That will rot you from the inside out.

This is: **expect neutral, practice honor anyway.**

For 24 hours, run this mental setting:

**Default expectation:** neutral (not worship, not war)

**Your standard:** honor + clear boundaries

### In Practice:

Give one person **unexpected respect** today:

sincere compliment
thank-you message
small service
public credit where it's due

Then write what happened:

**Their response:**

**My internal reaction:**

**What this teaches me about expectations:**

You're training your brain to stop demanding, and to start receiving.

## Day 7 — Follow-Through or Fantasy (Lock it in)

Pick **one standard** you created.
Make it real with consequences.

Complete these honestly:

**My standard is:**

**I will do it on:**

**If I miss twice in a row, I will:**

**Example:** "restart with 2 minutes tonight + text my candle."

## The Fires of Yesterday

Write one expectation you're releasing.
Read it out loud.

Then say:

**"I release the script. I keep the standard. I trust God with outcomes."**

Tear it up/delete it/burn it (safely, not arson-y).

**End of Week (Summary):**

Agreements spoken:

Boundaries set:

Standards installed:

Ninja expectations exposed:

Disappointment episodes reduced (estimate): %

# Wrapping Up

So fuck it.
Release them.

Live freer.
Flow lighter.

Trust God—let go of the rest.

***"Cast thy burden upon the LORD, and he shall sustain thee: he shall never suffer the righteous to be moved."*** (Psalm 55:22, KJV)

Ditching expectations feels counterintuitive—scary—even. Because expectations give a false sense of control: the illusion that if we can predict the outcome, we can protect ourselves from pain.

I struggled with it too.

I used to think expectations were standards—that they showed I cared.

But what they really gave me was anxiety.
Disappointment. Resentment.

Letting go of a mass majority of expectations brought me peace.

And I'll be honest.
They still creep back in sometimes.

Especially dealing with the deep desires of the flesh:
Money. Sex. Work. Respect. Compassion. Unconditional love.

Expectations are heavy.
They anchor you to "shoulda coulda woulda," as my dad always said.

The demon of the Past whispers, *"It would have been better if..."*
The demon of the Future screams, *"You should be there by now."*

But grace doesn't live in shouldas, couldas, or wouldas.

Grace lives in surrender.

Fuck it.
Release them.

Let go of the timelines.
The outcomes.
The picture-perfect version of how you thought your story should, would, or could go.

Because life rarely unfolds according to your script. And that's the point...you're not even the director.

You're only the main character.

# Chapter 7

# Fvck 100% Positivity

**Ego Alert:** "Good vibes only" is spiritual makeup on emotional rot. It's not healing—it's hiding.

**Vow:** I tell the truth without theatrics. I heal for real.

## Positive Vibes Only

We now live in a culture obsessed with “good vibes only.”

Scroll social and it’s plastered everywhere—smiles, affirmations, the relentless demand to “look on the bright side.”

**The real truth** is it’s a bullshit way to live.

Yeah, I said it.

Negativity is real.
Pain is real.

And pretending otherwise doesn’t bring you any closer to a more healed version of you—it **pressurizes you**.

Life is not meant to be 100% sunshine and gratitude journals while we shart out rainbows and sneeze fairy dust in people’s face.

“Good vibes only” isn’t pure positivity—**it’s emotional censorship**.

It trains you to hide grief behind a grin, to call trauma a “lesson” before the bruise has even formed, to label anger as “bad” instead of recognizing it as a boundary that needs honoring.

That’s not healthy.

That’s dishonest.

# FVCK 100% POSITIVITY

Let's call it what it is:

**Toxic positivity**—optimism cosplaying as healthy while your soul quietly suffocates behind the scenes.

**Optimism** says: "There's hope."

**Toxic Positivity** says: "There's only hope—shut up with your sadness."

**Honesty** says: "There's pain and there's hope. I'll tell the truth and take the next faithful step."

Even Scripture refuses "good vibes only."

Ecclesiastes tells us there is a time to weep and a time to laugh.

The Psalms are basically a playlist of lament and praise.

Jesus wept; and if the Son of God can cry shamelessly, you can stop expecting yourself—and everyone around you—to smile 24/7...stop apologizing for not being "upbeat" when you don't feel upbeat.

A sunshine-only garden grows shallow roots.
The first drought kills it.

Plants deepen roots from storms and shade. You don't get resilience from a ring light; you get it from weathering anything you face that is real.

Let's put a name on a healthy alternative: **holy realism**.

Not despair. Not denial.
Reality with God in it.

You don't have to pretend you're okay to be faithful.
You don't have to slap a smile on a wound to be "strong."

Sometimes the **most spiritual** thing you can say is:
"This hurts. I'm not okay. And I am still here."

Here's what *"positive vibes only"* really does:
**it makes pain feel like a personal failure.**

Like if you were "better," you'd be happier.
That's a flat out lie that turns your suffering into shame.

Life is **both/and:**
**You can be grateful and grieving.**
**You can be helpful and exhausted.**
**You can love someone and deny access.**

If your emotions are a storm, positivity-only culture tells you to deny the storm.

**Holy realism says:** name it, shelter wisely, and keep moving.

Your feelings don't make you unworthy.
They make you human.

Constant happiness isn't possible. Yet, people are making it a mission in life. The goal isn't a perma-smile.

The goal is integrity—being one whole person.

One whole package of authenticity.
Not a performance—and this is why...

## The Role of Negativity

Negativity, like everything else in life, serves a purpose.

We're talking about energy here. A Universal truth regardless of your religious faith.

Quit trying to cancel it.
The goal is to handle it with grace.

### 1) Acknowledge it:

Suppressing negative emotion doesn't erase it; it pressurizes it. Lab work shows suppression jacks up physiological arousal (heart rate, blood pressure) and makes feelings rebound harder (**Gross & Levenson, 1997**). Broader reviews link chronic suppression to worse mental health and relationship outcomes (see meta-analytic trends like Aldao et al., 2010).

**Translation:** stuffing it now means paying interest on it later.

### 2) Name it:

Neuroscience shows that affect labeling—putting a word on your feeling—quiets the amygdala (fear hub) and recruits prefrontal control (Lieberman et al., 2007).

**Translation:** call your shit what it is, and it loosens its grip.

### 3) Redirect it:
Negative emotions are data that can drive wise action...

**Anger**, when channeled correctly, is a primer for setting boundaries and pursuing justice (Harmon-Jones & Allen, 1998; Carver & Harmon-Jones, 2009).

**Frustration** flags a mismatch—something needs to change (process, standard, boundary).

**Sadness** can deepen empathy and connection; shared sorrow bonds people (Keltner & Gross, 1999).

The point isn't to wallow; it's to aim.

### 4) Reframe it

Cognitive reappraisal—telling a truer, bigger story about what happened—reduces negative affect and physiological load (Gross, 1998/2002).

Reframe doesn't mean "pretend it's fine."
It means: *This hurts* **and** *here's what it invites me to do next.*

Even Jesus didn't sugarcoat life:

***"These things I have spoken unto you, that in me ye might have peace. In the world ye shall have tribulation: but be of good cheer; I have overcome the world."*** (John 16:33, KJV)

He didn't say "think positive vibes only."
He said expect trouble—and take heart anyway.

Ope! Paradox:
The moment you label someone else "negative,"—whether you say it for all to hear or just in your head—you yourself are being negative.

So check yourself on putting labels on other's.
You worry about your own labels.

Can we normalize giving negativity space?

## Giving Negativity Space

Sometimes the most positive thing you can do is ***let*** yourself be negative for a moment.

Go on a rant.
Cry it out.
Vent to someone who won't take it personally but you also trust to call you out on bullshit within your negativity.

It's helpful to have external checks and balances for your emotions and vibes (Hi therapy).

Set the scene before you go ape shit about anything; it's a pressure valve that releases steam safely before it overpressurizes.

Even Scripture makes a point of instructing us to get shit off our chest honestly:

***"How long wilt thou forget me, O LORD? for ever? how long wilt thou hide thy face from me?"***
(Psalm 13:1, KJV)

That's not "good vibes only."

That's raw honesty. And it's holy.

## Where Negativity Works (and where it can go wrong)

**Expressive writing** helps.
Studies on writing about painful experiences show improvements in mental and even physical health over time (Pennebaker & Beall; Smyth meta-analyses).

**Translation:** structured disclosure reduces the pressure in the system.

**Label + feel beats bottle + burst.**
Naming the emotion reduces amygdala reactivity (affect labeling), while bottling it spikes physiological stress.

**But unstructured venting** can backfire.

Pure rumination keeps anger hot, and "catharsis" by hitting things and slamming doors tends to ***increase*** aggression.

So: **release, don't rehearse.**
Lament, don't loop.

# The Farmer's Fortune

There was once an old farmer in a small village.

He wasn't rich, but he had a horse that helped him plow the fields. One day, the horse broke through the gate and ran away into the hills.

The neighbors rushed over, clucking their tongues:
*"What terrible luck! Now you'll never get your work done."*

The farmer just shrugged and said: *"Maybe."*

A week later, the horse returned.
This time bringing with it a herd of wild horses. Suddenly the farmer had more horses than anyone in the village.

The neighbors ran over again:
*"What amazing luck! You have so many you're rich now!"*

Again the farmer said: *"Maybe."*

Not long after, the farmer's son was working one of the wild horses to tame. The horse bucked him off, and the boy broke his leg.

The neighbors rushed over yet again:
*"What awful luck! Your only son is crippled! You're ruined."*

But the farmer simply said again: *"Maybe."*

A month later, soldiers came to the village to draft every able-bodied young man for war. But the farmer's son, with his broken leg, was left at home.

This time the neighbors said nothing.

What looks negative today may turn positive tomorrow. And what looks positive may come with its own hidden load of negativity.

Life swings back and forth, and the truth is, you rarely know in the moment what the bigger picture really means.

The farmer's wisdom wasn't into predicting outcomes to be good or bad.

He was into remaining steady and not clinging too tightly to either despair or celebration.

**Just wait and see.**

Scripture teaches the same principle:

***"And we know that all things work together for good to them that love God, to them who are the called according to his purpose."*** (Romans 8:28, KJV)

"All things" in that verse means: the runaway horse, the broken leg, the unexpected blessing of the son not going to war, and even the pain through it all.

The farmer's *"Maybe,"* echoes the call to trust that every twist, every turn, is part of a bigger story we will never see until it unfolds.

## Job's Trials: Faith Isn't a Filter

If anybody could stand in a courtroom and call bullshit on "good vibes only," it was Job.

Job wasn't some slouch. The man had it all—wealth, family, reputation, security. Then the storm hit.

One messenger showed up, dust in his hair, panic in his eyes:
*"Raiders stole your oxen and donkeys. Your servants are dead."*

Before Job could breathe, another stumbled in:
*"Fire from the sky burned up your sheep and the shepherds."*

Then another:
*"The Chaldeans raided, your camels are gone."*

And the final gut punch:
*"A mighty wind collapsed the house where your sons and daughters were feasting. They're dead."*

One after another.
Four wrecking balls in a row.

Imagine losing your business, your livelihood, your family.
All in a single day.
And Job dropped to the ground.

Not in defeat.
But in worship.

*"The Lord gave, and the Lord has taken away. Blessed be the name of the Lord."*

But it didn't stop there.

Satan struck his body. Head to toe, painful sores. Job sat in the ashes, scraping his skin with broken pottery just to get relief.

Imagine the smell of infection, the sting of open wounds, the humiliation of neighbors watching him rot.

And his wife?
Instead of comfort, she hissed: *"Do you still hold fast to your integrity? Curse God and die."*

His friends arrived.
At first, they sat silent with him for seven days and nights, which was the best thing they could've done. A tradition to allow time to mourn.

But then they opened their mouths and ruined it.
Blaming him. Accusing him. Telling him he must've sinned.

Job didn't fake it.

He didn't paste a smile on his blistered face and chant affirmations.

He wept.
He cursed the day of his birth.
He screamed at heaven.

But—and this is the difference—he didn't walk away from God.

He wrestled with Him.
He stayed in the fight.

And when the dust settled, when God finally answered out of the whirlwind, Job saw the truth: he wasn't abandoned.

He was refined.
His ending was richer than his beginning.
Family restored. Fortune doubled.

His story is immortalized.

The lesson?

Life is not "good vibes only."
It's fire and ashes. Screams and silence. Loss and restoration.

Faith isn't pretending life is flawless.
Faith is still clinging to God in the dark.

We just opened a pressure valve with lamentation. There's another valve available when you need it: humor.

## Humor in the Darkness

I don't mean using humor as a mask to hide emotional pain—but I don't know of any better medicine.

Life gets ridiculous.
Personally, I fart in public. Often.
I still laugh about it—and I refuse to let shame bully me into holding in gas like it's a virtue.

Humor isn't childish; it's survival.

Psychologists call this a kind of **positive reappraisal**—reframing a negative moment with humor to drop stress and boost resilience (Martin, 2007).

That fart?
Not an embarrassment. It's freedom.

Even the Bible admits it: sorrow refines us more than laughter.

That doesn't make laughter useless.
It means you can't laugh your way through every storm.

Humor is a release valve; sorrow is a forge.

One keeps you alive; the other makes you grow.
And you need both.

The psych side backs this both/and:

**Self-enhancing humor** (laughing *with* yourself, not *at* yourself) is linked to better coping and lower distress; aggressive/self-defeating humor (at others' or your own expense) predicts worse outcomes (Martin et al., 2003).

**Translation:** use humor to connect, not to deflect or attack.

But bypassing pain with jokes—to keep pain underground. Feelings you refuse to feel won't disappear—they'll wait.

*"When Jesus heard of it, he departed thence by ship into a desert place apart: and when the people had heard thereof, they followed him on foot out of the cities."* (Matthew 14:13, KJV)

## Keep Humor Honest

Is this joke to connect or to avoid?

**If avoid:** give yourself 120 seconds of truth (say it / write it), then joke if you want.

**If connect:** share the laugh, then take one next faithful step (text the check-in, pray a Psalm, step outside).

**Humor = valve**
**Lament = forge**

Use both—on purpose.

And remember **Jesus**:
When grief hit, He didn't perform.
He withdrew. He grieved.
Then he moved in compassion toward the people.

Laugh when you can.
But don't fear the tears for the sake of keeping the vibes high.

***"Even in laughter the heart is sorrowful; and the end of that mirth is heaviness."*** (Proverbs 14:13, KJV)

Positive.
Negative.

When you're working with both—when you're letting the energies match the emotions and the feelings.
There can be a harmonious flow to life.
***There can be power in polarity.***

## Both/And: Power in Polarity

Like yin and yang, like a battery has negative and positive terminals.

No polarity, no current.
Life is the same.

Life is both/and, not either/or.

Scripture calls it seasons:

***"A time to weep, and a time to laugh; a time to mourn, and a time to dance;"*** (Ecclesiastes 3:4, KJV)

In the real disillusioned world—positivity and negativity are both given the space they need.

Both belong righteously.

Resilience isn't staying in one gear; the flex is being able to shift between them.

All sunshine? Shallow roots.
All storms? Uprooted.

**Sun + storms = deep roots.**

We named the two poles.
Now let's talk about what the **storm** actually does to you.

After all—there ***will always*** be storms.

## When Negativity Teaches (and when it doesn't)

In hindsight, the hardest seasons—the ugly, messy, negative ones—are the ones that force the most growth.

Not because pain is good but because pain reveals truth.

When it shows itself to you.
Do your best not numb the pain—or neglect it—because friction is what creates the edge of a blade.

***"Iron sharpeneth iron; so a man sharpeneth the countenance of his friend."*** (Proverbs 27:17, KJV)

**Important caveat:** I'm not glamorizing trauma.

Some wounds are catastrophic and need time, treatment, and tenderness.

Growth isn't guaranteed; nor is it ever linear; nor is there ever a graduation from healing school.

It is possible though—especially when you tie pain up with honesty, professional help, and staying focused on the next faithful steps.

You are not alone.

# The Crow and the Pitcher

It was the peak of summer, hot as hell out, and a crow was dying of thirst. He spotted a pitcher sitting outside a farmhouse.

He flew to it with hope in his heart.
But when he looked inside, there was only a little bit of water pooled at the very bottom.

He stretched his neck, jabbed his beak, tried every angle, but he couldn't reach it.

Frustration hit hard.

He could've cursed the world, kicked the dirt, and flown off to die. But instead, he stopped.

He thought for a second while he looked around.
Then he spotted some small stones scattered nearby.

One by one, the crow picked up the stones in his beak and dropped them into the pitcher.

Slowly, the water level began to rise.

He kept at it, dropping stone after stone, until finally the water was high enough for him to drink.

His thirst was quenched.

Not because luck handed him what he needed, but because he faced the frustration, got creative, and turned a negative into a solution.

## A Personal Wake-Up Call

I'll never forget it. 2019, walking the streets of Seattle with a close friend. I was ranting—marriage, business, life—as everything felt like it was crumbling.

He stopped me mid-sentence: "When did you get so negative?" He wasn't judging; he was concerned. And he was right.

Negativity had taken over the whole stage.

That moment reminded me:
**negativity has a place—but not as the leading role.**

**Life fact:** There will always be both positivity and negativity.

**Life fact:** What matters is what you choose in each moment—then how you move from there.

**Life fact:** Life will feel like a pile of shit sometimes.
Remember—compost comes from piles of shit.
It usually stinks before it grows anything you want to eat.

**Life fact:** Some of humanity's greatest accomplishments were born in and out of negative circumstances. Penicillin from mold, civil rights movements from oppression, strength forged out of grief.

Even Jesus framed it for us:

***"Blessed are the poor in spirit: for theirs is the kingdom of heaven. Blessed are they that mourn: for they shall be comforted."*** (Matthew 5:4-5, KJV)

Mourning isn't a weakness.
It's an opening to deeper strength.

# Field Work:
# The 7 Day "Weather Report"

***(Make this chapter real. Not pretty.)***

## 1) Three moves when the dark shows up

**Allow:** *"This is anger/grief/fear. It's real."*

**Align:** Inhale 4, exhale 6, 6–8 cycles.

**Ask:** *"What matters here—truth, love, courage, justice?"*
(Psych flexibility = feel fully, act by values.)

**Act:** one **faithful** step you can do now:
text the apology, pray Psalm 13/27/51, step outside for 3 minutes, drink water, write 3 honest lines, set one boundary, deadlift, take a shower.

## 2) Use the right tool for the right storm

**Overwhelm → Ground** (5–4–3–2–1 senses + 4–6 breathing)

**Spin/rumination → Reframe** (*"This is a chapter, not the book."*)

**Anxiety avoidance → Approach** (one tiny step toward the thing you fear)

**Injustice/anger → Channel** (name the wrong + one non-destructive action)

**Numbness → Engage** (movement, sunlight, a call—behavior precedes mood)

### 3) Don't do this

**Suppress** ("I'm fine") → spikes physiology, rebounds harder.

**Bypass** (platitudes to dodge pain) → pain goes underground.

**Compare** ("Others have it worse") → invalidates and stalls healing.

**Loop** (endless venting) → rehearses the wound without resolving it.

### 4) Seven-day field test

Each day, write two lines:

**Emotion (1 word)** + **Body cue** (tight chest, hot face, hollow gut).

**Next faithful step** you did (one sentence).

Add one checkbox for each day.

Seven boxes = data that your honesty **moves** you, not ruins you.

## 5) When to bring in reinforcements

If the darkness is **persistent** (weeks), **global** ("everything is ruined"), or **intrusive** (sleep/appetite tanked, work/relationships impaired), get help.

That's wisdom, not weakness.

(If you're in the U.S. and it's acute, call/text **988**; elsewhere, use local crisis lines.)

## 6) 15-second prayer you can keep in your pocket

*Lord, this hurts.*
*I'm here.*
*You're here.*
*Show me the next faithful step.*
*I'll take it.*
*Amen.*

**Bottom line:** No rainbow chasing. You're learning **weather**—naming the sky, walking with God, and taking the next step.

That's not fluff.
That's formation.

When the sun is shining though.
Fucking let it shine my friend.

## Wrapping Up

So fuck it.

Stop chasing 100% positivity.

Stop shaming yourself for having a moment of negativity.

Stop shaming anyone else for their moments of negativity.

Negativity isn't weakness. Nor is it failure.

It's feedback.

For fuck... it's only the body's—and soul's—way of saying, ***"Something's off. Something needs attention."***

The goal isn't to erase negativity.
It's to learn to dance with it—to let it move through you, refine you, and teach you balance.

Light without shadow isn't light at all. It's blindness.

Without contrast, we can't see form, truth, or direction.

The same God who created the day also crafted the night.

Both serve a purpose.

Both reveal something about who we are...

Who ***He*** is.

And what's one of His favorite lines to say?

***"Do not be afraid."***
***"Do not fear."***

And courage so happens to be the root for how we grow next.

# Chapter 8

# Fvck Your Fears

**Ego Alert:** Fear will paint your future like a crime scene and call it "being realistic."

**Vow:** I move while I'm afraid.

## Fear: The Silent Killer

Fear is the disease almost no one wants to talk about—and fewer actually touch. I'm not talking about the classic phobias—spiders, tight spaces, heights—as real as those are.

But I'm talking about a ***different*** kind of fear.

I'm talking about the fear that strangles your potential in the dark:

Fear of **failure**.

Fear of **success**—what it will demand...who it will expose.

Fear of **abandonment**—once you step into who you were called to be.

The fear that paralyzes your soul. Your greatest self.
It steals opportunities, sabotages relationships, wrecks your health, and leaves you muttering regrets on your deathbed.

**Fear is a thief.**
It doesn't have to knock you out; it just has to keep you on the couch. Scrolling. Dreaming.

Waiting for "the right moment."

Fear doesn't just say, "*Hey you. With the ambition. Stop.*"
Fear gets creative.
It learns your voice. Your logic.

Fear conspires alongside the Ego and crafts Oscar-worthy performances.

It'll say:
***"Maybe you should wait until you're actually ready."***
**Translation:** never gonna fucking happen.

*"Maybe now isn't the right time."*
**Translation:** stay safe.

*"Maybe you're being unrealistic."*
**Translation:** stay small—small is also safe.

Do this: **Fear Receipts**

Write down the questions and answer them:

*What am I afraid will happen?*
*What's the realistic probability of this actually happening?*
*If it does happen, what can I do about it?*
(actual steps, not just vibes.)

Fear is afraid of steps.
Fear loves fog.

And then—this is important—define the real danger:
Is it physical danger?
Danger to the Ego?
Is it a true risk—or just a discomfort outside my safe zone?

Most of what paralyzes people isn't a threat to their life.

It’s rarely about actual death or injury.
It’s usually about embarrassment—at any level.

It’s a threat to their identity. Their Ego.

So choose your pain—because pain is going to be involved regardless of which direction you choose:

The pain of discipline.
Or the pain of regret.

One builds you.
One buries you.

And if you don’t confront it, fear wins by default.
Without ever having to lift a finger.

So let's drag this slimy, corrupt, bastard into the light.

**Fuck.**

**Your.**

**Fears.**

## The Thief’s Trick (and how to break it)

Fear isn’t going to suddenly flip your life upside down. It latches on like a parasite and feeds off you until completely undetected.

This is precisely why I said in the beginning of the chapter how this is a different kind of fear.

It's doesn't have you jumping onto the counters.

It works on you subtly and without warning; you're flipping your own life upside down.

It keeps you from sending the message, applying for the role, having the conversation, or stepping into the room—you'll never know what was on the other side until it's too late.

So we're doing two things:

**Shrink the monster** (name it, normalize it, right-size it).

**Build a ladder** (micro-steps that teach your nervous system: "I can handle this").

# Fear Ladder

# (exposure with swagger)

### 1) Name the dragon:

One sentence.

No drama: *"I'm afraid if I ask for a raise, my boss will get mad."*

### 2) Rate it:

Write the number.

From 0 to 10...Proof beats pep talks.

### 3) Build a three-rung ladder:

**Rung 1 (easy):** the smallest exposure (draft the post title; outline the pitch; text one safe friend).

**Rung 2 (medium):** a public but low-risk action (share with one group; submit to one gatekeeper).

**Rung 3 (real):** the thing (publish, apply, ask, walk in).

### 4) If–then the start line:

*If* it's **6:00 p.m.**, *then* I do **Rung 1 for 2 minutes**.

No feelings get a vote. This is an Executive Order.

### 5) Do Rung 1 now:

When you finish, re-rate fear. If the number dropped even one point, you just proved the rule: approach shrinks fear.

Repeat tomorrow.
Add a rung when you're ready.

**This is exposure with swagger.**

## The Faith Move

Fear's favorite costume is "prudence."
It'll call itself "waiting for the right time," "needing clarity," or "protecting my peace."

Sometimes that's wisdom; a lot of times it's ego avoidance. Scripture cuts clean:

*"Fear thou not; for I am with thee: be not dismayed; for I am thy God: I will strengthen thee; yea, I will help thee; yea, I will uphold thee with the right hand of my righteousness."*
(Isaiah 41:10, KJV)

*"For God hath not given us the spirit of fear; but of power, and of love, and of a sound mind."*
(2 Timothy 1:7, KJV)

**Power** = you can take the step.

**Love** = you can take it for the right reasons.

**Self-control** = you can take it on purpose.

## Fear Audit:

**What fear is this—really?**
(*failure/success/abandonment/exposure/uncertainty*)

**What's the smallest honest step?**
(*Rung 1?*)

**Who gets the check-in text/pic?**
(*one witness from your Five*)

**When do I do it?**
(*timestamp*)

**Prayer:** "*Lord, I'm afraid. Thank you for guiding my steps and illuminating my path. I'm moving in faith. I trust your work.*"

The thief was identified.

Now let's zoom in on its wiring—**what fear does to your brain and body,** and how to hit the brakes.

## Neurons Under Siege

Fear isn't just "in your head."
It's in your ***whole body***.

Your amygdala is the brain's alarm.
When it senses danger, it hijacks your nervous system and launches ***fight, flight, freeze, or fawn***.

What once kept you alive when a lion rustled through the bushes—now lights up when you think about quitting your job, leaving a toxic relationship, or starting the business you've been dreaming about.

Fear ***exaggerates*** the threat:
It makes the lion bigger.
The storm stronger.
The risk riskier.

Whether the threat is real or imagined, your body reacts the same: pounding heart, sweaty palms, stomach in knots.

Long-term, chronic fear will fucking wreck you.
It's not poetic either.

Prolonged stress hormones (like cortisol) are linked to **hippocampal atrophy** (memory/learning) and **weakened prefrontal control** (planning, judgment) (McEwen, 2007; Arnsten, 2009).

**Translation:** live in fear long enough and you literally rewire yourself to be —more sick, more rundown, more forgetful, and irritable as fuck.

That's why fear doesn't just steal today—it poisons tomorrow.

## Why Fear Feels Bigger Than It Is

**Your brain over-detects threats.**
Survival math, not moral failure.

**Avoidance feeds fear.**
Avoidance works **now**, **smaller** life later.

**Action rewires fear.**
Stepwise exposure teaches *feared ≠ fatal.*

**Uncertainty is the drug.**
Approaching the **unknown** starves fear of its favorite food.

**Translation:** fear **screams**, avoidance **feeds** it, **small brave acts** starve it.

***"What time I am afraid, I will trust in thee. In God I will praise his word, in God I have put my trust; I will not fear what flesh can do unto me."***
(Psalm 56:3–4, KJV)

Not ***if*** I am afraid—when.
Feel it. Choose trust.

Move.

We know fear is a shitty chemistry teacher—and a liar.

Now let's spot how it **acts** in real life so you can cut its cords.

## Fear's Four Faces (and a counter-attack)

These are the F's that fear uses to fuck you. They may show up in more areas of your life than you think:

### Fight:

Your spouse or coworker snaps at you for making a mistake—you want to get snippy because you doing your best.

**Body:** 4-6 deep breaths for 6-8 cycles
**Mind:** name the fear ("I'm afraid I'll be rejected.")

**Mouth:** one calm boundary ("I won't be yelled at. Let's try again after a 30 minute cool-down. I want to solve this.")

## Flight:

You ghost the opportunity, cancel the interview, avoid the hard conversation.

**Timer:** 2 minutes
**Action:** smallest approach step only (open the doc, draft the subject line, schedule the call.)
**Rule:** when the timer ends, you can stop (but you can keep going too.)

## Freeze:

You parked in analysis paralysis. You **know** the next step...but never move.

**Countdown:** 3...2...1...go (stand up, put on shoes)
**One-Inch Action:** 1 sentence, 1 email, 1 push-up, 1 minute
**If-Then:** "If it's 6:00pm, then I'll do 1 minute." Non-negotiable.

## Fawn:

You people-please, over-explain, and sell yourself short **just** to keep the peace.

**Script:** "I can do X. I can't do Y. If Z is required, I'm out."
**Pause:** Before and After you speak.

Fear doesn't care which option you choose. As long as one of the Four Fs of Fear's Fuckery keeps you from your greatness.

It doesn't care whether you win or lose, are happy or sad, or successful.

It only cares about one thing and one thing only—that ***you don't move forward with your soul.***

It's happy with that soul-sucking paycheck.

**Warning:** All four can get **negatively reinforced**.

This is because they bring fast relief now.
Your brain learns to repeat them later—*when* you find yourself in similar situation.

**Bottom line:** notice your Fear Fuck, run the play, take the step.

Fear loses the second you move.

### One-Liner Prayer

"Lord, I'm afraid. Remove any stumbling blocks from my path—and I'll continue to take faithful steps."

## Faith Over Fear

Fear and faith are opposites.
Where one lives. The other dies.

And let me make this perfectly clear:
Faith isn't the absence of fear.
Faith is obedience to move through the presence of fear.

So when we say "faith and fear can't coexist," what we really mean is: they can't both be in the driver's seat at the same time.

God's hall of fame is full of scared people who moved anyway: Moses, Gideon, Esther, Peter—hell, even Jesus in Gethsemane under the weight of what was coming.

That's not fearlessness.
That's surrender while shaking.

And yes—you'll hear people say the Holy Bible says "do not fear" 365 times, one for every day of the year. The exact count is messy—messier than the meme—but the point still stands:

Scripture doesn't whisper courage once.
It repeats it like a teacher drills math equations into your memory bank.

## Where Fear Hides In Real Life

Fear doesn't just live in the "big moments."

It dwells in your daily patterns too.

These are more difficult to recognize and pinpoint the sources of the stronghold. Here's some common places we can search for this sneaky fucker.

**Money:** Fear chains you to a paycheck that kills your soul.

*What's happening:* **Status quo bias** + **loss aversion**—you overweigh what you might lose and underweigh what you might gain. Sunk costs keep you stuck

*Antidote:* Build a **3–6 month runway** (start with one month).
Apply to **two** roles/week.
Start a **1-hour/week** skill-up or side project.
Make a **stop rule**: *If* X conditions aren't met by Y date, *then* I pivot.

**Love:** Fear convinces you it's better to be abused than alone.

*What's happening:* **Attachment wounds** + "scarcity story" (no one else will want me). Trauma bonds reward short-term relief.

*Antidote:* Write a **non-negotiable boundary**: *"If X happens, I leave/call for help."* Tell one trusted person. Create a **safety plan** and stash cash/docs.

(**If you're in danger**: in the U.S. dial **911** for immediate emergencies.
Otherwise, call/text **988** or
**National Domestic Violence Hotline 800-799-7233**;
use local resources elsewhere.)

**Parenting:** Fear makes you overprotective—raising kids who never learn resilience.

*What's happening:* Overprotection blocks **competence**; kids need manageable risk to grow.

*Antidote:* Practice **scaffolded risk**—one age-appropriate challenge/week (order at restaurant, bike to park, solve a peer conflict).
Praise **effort/strategy**, not perfection. Debrief failures as data.

**Leadership:** Fear turns bosses into micromanagers.

*What's happening:* You crush **autonomy**, killing motivation (Self-Determination Theory). Teams go silent.

*Antidote:* Create **psychological safety** (Edmondson)—set a **clear standard**, ask one *specific* learning question per meeting, and **thank dissent**.
Delegate outcomes with a **check-in cadence** (not constant pings).

**Creativity:** Fear kills ideas before they're born.

*What's happening:* **Evaluation anxiety** + perfectionism. Your inner critic shoots drafts on the runway.

*Antidote:* Run **quantity over quality** sprints: 10 bad ideas in 10 minutes. Write a **shitty first draft** on purpose. Protect maker time (90-minute block, notifications off).

Share **one** thing weekly.

**Bottom line:** Fear is death in the slowest, most painful, decaying way—**unless** you starve it with small, honest moves.

# The Cost of Fear

Bronnie Ware, a hospice nurse, asked dying patients about their regrets. The most common:
"I wish I'd had the courage to live a life true to myself, not the life others expected of me."

Notice the word: **courage.**
Not talent.
Not money.
Not luck.

Courage.

Fear leaves you whispering "what if."
Courage leaves you shouting "fuck yeah!"

Psychologists have proven it: people regret inaction far more than mistakes. We fear loss more than we desire gain (Kahneman & Tversky).

That's why fear works.

It exaggerates the risk of losing. But over decades, 84% of regret people carry are about the chances they didn't take, not the ones they did (Gilovich & Medvec).

Fear makes you hesitate.

Regret makes you rot.

Courage gives you good works and a smile.

## Field Work: How to Fuck Your Fears

Let's get tactical.
Here's how you fight back:

**Name It**:
Write the fear down. Drag it out of your head and onto paper. Clarity shrinks monsters.

**Worst Case Scenario**:
Write out the absolute worst that could happen.
Most of the time—you realize you'll survive.

**Fear Ladder**:
Take baby steps.
Afraid of public speaking? Start with two people.
Then five. Then twenty.
Exposure rewires your brain.

**Fear Journal**:
Track every time fear stops you.
Then write how you'll confront it tomorrow.

**Scriptural Affirmations**:
Declare truth out loud.
*"The Lord is my light and salvation, whom shall I fear?"*

**Accountability**:
Surround yourself with people who won't let you bullshit yourself.

Lone wolves can get eaten alive.

## Wrapping Up

Fear never fully leaves you alone.
Always plotting in tandem with the Ego.

You can pray it down, fight back against it, meditate quietly with it, but it never dies.

And maybe that's the point. Because fear was never the enemy to begin with.

Fear was designed to be a *compass*.
We just forgot how to make sense of it's directional input.

The issue is—most people run in the direction *opposite* of where the compass points. This chapter is here to convince you to run in the direction the compass is pointing.

Toward fear.

Not because you're reckless—but because you're alive and ready to thrive.

Greatness is found on the other side of fear.
Do it scared.
Do it shaking.
Do it messy.

Feel it and do it anyway.

## FVCK YOUR FEARS

Because courage isn't the absence of fear.
It's dragging fear with you by the hair while it kicks and screams for you to stop.

Courage, then, is the art of interpretation…or rather…reinterpretation.

It's looking fear in the face and saying, "Thank you for the warning but I'm still going full send."

That's faith.
That's obedience.
That's more than *being* alive.

It's taking advantage of life.

So here's your call:

Fuck your fears.

Not by fighting them, not by fleeing from them.

By making those fucks afraid of you.

Now we face the fear most people baptize as "wisdom," "responsibility," or "status": **Money.**

# Chapter 9

# Fvck Money

**Ego Alert:** Money will try to become your god—then punish you with anxiety either way.

**Vow:** I am the master of my tools. I don't worship them.

# ChaChing

The thing almost everyone wants more of but no one can seem to get enough of. No number big enough to satiate the hunger and desire most feel toward it.

The silent obsession of our age. It hides in every advertisement, fuels every scam, manipulates nearly every sale, and feeds every addiction.

Lottery tickets.
Wall Street greed.
Corporate fraud.
Drugs.
Sex.
Sports.

You name it—money is in the middle of it.

But let's be brutally honest: money ***isn't*** the problem.

**Our *relationship* to money is the fucking problem.**

Money is a magnifier.

It doesn't make you good or evil—it only turns the volume up to what's already within you.

The greedy become greedier.
The generous become more generous.
Fear becomes louder.

Wisdom does too.
It's always been about what's inside you.

The real work isn't to get more money.
It's to get a new mirror.

**Money Mirror:** Write down the questions and answer them

***When I think about money, what do I feel first—fear, shame, pride, control, scarcity?***

***Who taught me that feeling?***

***What do I believe money will finally give me—security, respect, freedom, love?***

(There's a bit more but first...)

For centuries, humanity has both worshiped and despised money in the same breath.

We've fought wars over it, enslaved nations for it, broken families in its name, and sold our integrity for it.

Yet, at the same time, it builds hospitals, funds charities, feeds the poor, rescues lives, and advances our own very existence.

Money is ***neutral***.

It's unbiased as fuck.

It doesn't have feelings.

It's the hands and hearts holding it which determine its legacy.

The Holy Bible is crystal clear about it:

***"For the love of money is the root of all evil: which while some coveted after, they have erred from the faith, and pierced themselves through with many sorrows."*** (1 Timothy 6:10, KJV)

Notice it ***doesn't say money is evil.***
It's the ***love of money***—the attachment, the obsession, the idolatry— that's where corruption of the heart begins.

Let me be blunt: **money is a tool**.
It's as much of a tool as a wrench is to a bolt.

**And I'll say this plainly:** If a tool runs your life, you don't have a life—you have a *leash*.

This isn't a manifesto to burn a hole your bank account.
It's a middle finger to the idolatry and anxiety that turn a neutral tool into your master.

***"No man can serve two masters: for either he will hate the one, and love the other; or else he will hold to the one, and despise the other. Ye cannot serve God and mammon."***
(Matthew 6:24, KJV)

Money is a terrible god...

and a useful servant.

**Pick one.**

**Servant Rules:** Stack these on top of the three questions above.

**Give something** (even small, but consistently).
**Save something** (automatic, boring, faithful).
**Spend intentionally** (not emotionally)..

Money is a tool.

Not a god.
Not a judge.
Not your father.

## What I mean by "Fuck Money"

Fuck worshiping it.
Fuck defining yourself by it.
Fuck letting it choose your job, your marriage, your sanity.
Fuck making every decision with a calculator and no conscience.

We're not anti-wealth.
We're anti-bondage.

## The Great Illusion: Scarcity

Most people live as though money is oxygen: scarce, fleeting, and always about to run out. That's the ***scarcity mindset***—one of the most expensive beliefs you can carry.

A mental trap that doesn't just influence how much you spend but how much you believe you're capable of creating (Mullainathan & Shafir, 2013).

It's not one or the other. It both/and.
Scarcity whispers: *"There's never enough. Life is expensive."*

And once you believe that story, your brain goes to work proving it right. It'll have you sabotage opportunities, undersell yourself, and spend emotionally... all to fulfill the prophecy of lack.

***"For as he thinketh in his heart, so is he: Eat and drink, saith he to thee; but his heart is not with thee."*** (Proverbs 23:7, KJV)

If you constantly think of yourself as broke, unworthy, or undeserving, then your life will bend to fit that belief.

Here's the truth no one tells you: **abundance is also a mindset.**

Not magic.
Not delusion.
Not "manifest a sick Lambo."

It's the decision to stop living like lack is your identity.

## The Brain on Money

Money hits the same **dopamine** circuits that light up for reward prediction and status.

Read that again: **status**.

That's why money isn't just about math.

It's emotion in a trench coat pretending to be logic. Here's what's behind the trench coat:

**Hedonic treadmill:** you adapt fast. Yesterday's raise becomes today's baseline; the bar moves once you reach it.

**Scarcity tax:** when money feels tight, your brain's **bandwidth** shrinks—you make worse choices because scarcity is eroding your logic.

**Comparison poison:** your brain is a ranking machine. One scroll and you're "behind"—even if you're fine.

**Shame loop:** debt, spending, or family money trauma can wire money to **threat**. Your amygdala fires at bank apps like they're lions.

**Translation:** money isn't evil; **confusion, comparison, and fear** are. It's why people can have a decent income and still feel like they're drowning.

Because the real addiction isn't money.
**It's what money promises.**

Safety.
Worth.
Relief.
Approval.
Control.

And that brings us to the lies money has us believing.

## Four Money Lies—Busted

**Lie #1: "More money = increased safety."**
**Truth:** Safety is diversified—faith, community, skill, health, runway. Money helps, but it isn't a fortress; it's **sandbags**.

**Lie #2: "More money = worth."**
**Truth:** Worth is ***Imago Dei***—the truth that you are made in the Image of God, stamped before you ever held your first dollar. Net worth can't inflate what God already stamped.

**Lie #3: "More money = happy."**
**Truth:** Happiness rises with meeting real needs, then returns will **diminish**. Purpose, relationships, and integrity carry the weight joy can't outsource.

**Lie #4: "Blessed = richer."**
**Truth:** Prosperity without character ruins people. Scripture praises **stewardship**, **generosity**, and **contentment**, not flexing.

***"Let your conversation be without covetousness; and be content with such things as ye have: for he hath said, I will never leave thee, nor forsake thee."*** (Hebrews 13:5, KJV)

Contentment isn't passive. It's power.
It's the ability to say:"Enough."

And "enough" is a sentence that terrifies the marketplace... because markets survive on your constant dissatisfaction with what you already have.

## Money, Fear, and Control

If you grew up with scarcity and lack, money becomes your **control drug**.
If you grew up with abundance and strings, money becomes your **approval scale**.

Either way, the heart posture is the same:
*"If I have at least this much, I'll be okay."*

That's **fear** dressed up as math.

**Faith reorders it:** *"I will be okay and I'm grateful for what I do have—and I will act wisely with what comes and what goes."*

## Money & Marriage (Or Partnerships): Three Sentences That Save Wars

**Vision:** "Money serves our **values** (list 3) not our image."

**Roles:** "You manage **X**, I manage **Y**; we review **monthly**."

**Rules:** "We check in on any spend over **$____**. No secrets, ever."

***"For where your treasure is, there will your heart be also."*** (Matthew 6:21, KJV)

Any other direction and it's like the saying goes: "It's always fun until someone gets hurt."

Make sure your treasure is aimed where you want your heart to go. And let me tell you—when it's aimed with Ego—it gets really expensive.

## If You're in a Hole (Start Now)

**List the debts** (smallest → largest) + minimums.

**Call three bills** (internet/phone/insurance) and negotiate—yes, it works.

**Pick one debt tactic:** snowball (behavioral win) or avalanche (math win).

**Text a witness** from your Five with a pic when you complete one step.

It isn't about hating money.
It's about unhooking your soul from it.

Serve God.
Steward money.

Sleep like someone who knows which is which.

## Childhood Programming

Let's rewind a bit...maybe a lot.

For many of us, the way we think about money didn't start with becoming an adult. It started with the conversations, or lack thereof, in our childhood homes.

Some of us were told:
"Don't ask people how much they make."
"Don't talk about money at the dinner table.
"Don't put all your money in one place."
"Don't sell things just because you need money for something else."

These little phrases sound harmless—but they carry a ton of weight.

And kids don't learn from what their parents say.
They learn from what their parents do.

If your parents fought over bills, you learned money equals conflict. If they stressed every payday, you learned money equals fear. If they bought flashy things to look successful, you learned money equals status.

Those types of programs run deep.

Left unchecked, they become the operating system of our adulthood.

That's why you can swear you'll "never be like them," and then wake up one day doing the same exact dance...

**just with different music.**

## More Word Power

The words you speak about money are seeds, and every seed grows. When you say:
*"I can't afford that."*
*"Life is expensive."*
*"I'll never have enough money."*

You're planting seeds for an abundance of lack.

Read that again.

An *abundance...*

*...of lack.*

You're building a wall between you and what's truly possible.

Keep saying it, and your brain hardwires it as truth.

Remember that brain thing from the chapter on expectations?

Yeah, ***confirmation bias*** applies here too—imagine that: your mind filters reality to reinforce what you believe.

So instead of *"I can't afford that."* Put it this way:

*"I choose not to spend money on that right now."*

Notice the difference?

One is self-defeating.
**The other is self-governing.**

One says you're powerless.
**The other says you're in control.**

Words matter because they reveal who's driving:

You...
or fear.

Besides, if you can learn to lose the emotions when you step into Cash's office—when you keep it based on logic and reason—you can see things more clearly.

You can weigh options without emotional interjections.

## Three Choices With Money

Strip money down to its core, and you can only ever do three things with it:

1. **Consume** – Buy things, use things, eat things.

2. **Invest** – Grow it, multiply it, put it to work.

3. **Give** – Release it to bless others.

Most people stop at consumption.

They work for money...then just spend it. Especially when a lot of people have their retirement "automated."

It's a hamster wheel: paycheck in, paycheck out.

If you only ever consume, you become nothing more than a consumer—enslaved to the very thing you think you control.

Investing is where freedom is built.
Giving is where love and gratitude shine.

I'm not going to rely on a company matched 401k. I'm not going to rely on a mattress of cash.

My reliance is to my Lord and Savior Jesus Christ, God, and the Holy Ghost.

And sometimes the difference between "blessings" and "bankruptcy" is one word: **patience.**

# The Goose With Golden Eggs

A farmer once owned a goose that laid a single golden egg every day. Each egg was worth a fortune, and for a time the farmer was content. But greed has a way of whispering its evil. The farmer grew restless.

*"Why wait? If one egg a day is good, then the treasure inside this goose must be even greater."*

So, in his impatience, he killed the goose.
Only to find nothing inside.

In his rush for wealth, he destroyed the very source of it.

Isn't that us?

We sacrifice our health for overtime.
We sacrifice our relationships chasing bigger paychecks.
We sacrifice joy in the name of hustle.

And in the end, we kill the goose.

We burn out, break down, and then wonder why life feels empty.

Money without patience is destruction.
Money without wisdom is ruin.

And if you think that's just an ancient fable—consider the modern Golden Goose...

**lottery winners.**

# Jackpot

Every so often, headlines share a tragic story:

Someone wins the lottery, pockets tens of millions, sometimes hundreds of millions, and then spirals into destruction and then, bankruptcy.

Jack Whittaker, who won $315 million in 2002. The largest lottery payout to date. At first, it seemed like a dream come true. But within a few years, he was bankrupt. His granddaughter and daughter both died under tragic circumstances (tied to drugs and excess). He faced lawsuits, theft, robberies, and finally personal ruin.

In an interview years later, he admitted: ***"I wish I'd torn up the ticket."***

Fuck!
Can you imagine!?

$315 million dollars. And it wrecked him.
Reminds me of the Rich Fool from Luke 12.

And he isn't one exception. It happens quite often apparently. Whether the true data is 20% or 50% or 70% of winners ending up broke or bankrupt...

One thing is clear about anyone acquiring that much money and finding themselves broke:

**Money doesn't change you. It reveals you by magnifying what's already there.**

If you're reckless, more money makes you more reckless.
If you're generous, more money multiplies your impact.
If you're insecure, more money deepens the hole.

The kick in the ass?

Sudden wealth proves that it is far better to learn ***how to live*** rich before you ***become*** rich.

Rich living isn't about sick cars, giant houses, or lavish vacations.

It's about habits.
Stewardship.
Self-control.
Patience.
Charity.
Love.

*"He that is faithful in that which is least is faithful also in much: and he that is unjust in the least is unjust also in much."* (Luke 16:10, KJV)

If you can't manage a little, more won't save you.

**It will fucking crush you.**

# The Miser and His Gold

Aesop tells of a miser who hoarded a stash of gold. Too afraid to use it, too greedy to share it, he just buried it deep in the ground.

Every day he would visit the hole, dig it up, admire his treasure, then bury it again.

He never spent a single coin.

Not on food.
Not for comfort.
No charity for others.

The gold became nothing more than an idol he worshiped in secret.

One day, a thief discovered the hiding place and stole it all. When the miser returned to find the hole empty, he collapsed in grief.

A neighbor, hearing his wails, asked,
*"Why are you mourning? You never used the gold anyway. You might as well have buried stones."*

The point is sharp: money that is worshiped but never used is no different from rocks.

Hoarded wealth is sterile. Money only has value when it flows; it nourishes, it builds, it invests, or it blesses others.

Otherwise—it's as empty as a false idol feeding you lies.

## The Consumption Lie

Here's another trap to be aware of—and it could, quite possibly, be one of the biggest lies of our existence:

Convenience is value.

I'm going to use food as an example—because it's what I am most educated on in regard to any market.

Marketing convinces us we're making smart choices,

"heart healthy,"
"whole grain,"
"low-fat,"

but most of it ***takes*** from our lives rather than ***adds*** to them.

Beside that—when they are taking something from it (think "low-fat") to make it "healthy" they have to add something (processed sugar) unhealthy to bring the flavor back.

The simple fact of the matter is: most food in our world today doesn't feed **life**, it feeds **death**.

Companies profit while your body—*and* your wallet—pay the ultimate price.

Chronic diseases (both preventable and reversible) become more and more prevalent every year.

Inflammation.
Immune system malfunctions.
Type-2 Diabetes.
Obesity.
Cancer.

Don't just take my word for it...even though you can.

A Harvard study (Mozaffarian et al., 2019) found that diets high in processed foods are directly linked to higher mortality, cardiovascular disease, and diabetes.

Research from the National Institutes of Health (Hall et al., 2019) showed that people who consumed ultra-processed foods ate about 500 calories more per day than those on unprocessed diets. Leading to rapid weight gain.

Globally, the World Health Organization has labeled processed foods and sugary drinks as major contributors to the rise of chronic disease.

**Translation, without the lab coat:** "Cheap" food is the most expensive purchase you can make...because the currency is your quality of life, and life itself.

The Bible warns us too:

***"Be not among winebibbers; among riotous eaters of flesh: For the drunkard and the glutton shall come to poverty: and drowsiness shall clothe a man with rags."*** (Proverbs 23:20–21, KJV)

Gluttony drains both your wallet and your body.

Not because God hates pleasure—because God hates bondage.

And addiction to consumables of any kind is just bondage with branding.

## Taking Responsibility

I don't hold a single grudge toward my parents. I believe they did the best they could with what they knew, and with what they had. Just as any good loving parents do for their kids.

And I'm highly thankful for all they did...and didn't do. But here's what I've learned: **we must own our lives.**

Of course—this won't apply to all people—but a lot of people are quick to blame others for their shortcomings:

The government.
Their parents.
Their boss.
Their friends.
Their trauma.
Their childhood.

Their pets.
Their astrological sign.
Mercury in retrograde.

Blame is a thief.

Responsibility is the only path to freedom.

Psychology calls it an ***internal locus of control***: the belief that your actions—not outside forces—determine your outcomes.

People with an internal locus of control are healthier, more resilient, and more successful across almost every area of life.

Those with an external locus of control—blaming anything else—suffer higher rates of anxiety, depression, and financial instability.

The Bible even whispers it:

***"For every man shall bear his own burden."***
(Galatians 6:5, KJV)

God calls us to take ownership, not outsource blame.

When Adam blamed Eve and Eve blamed the serpent, humanity fell.

Responsibility restores power.

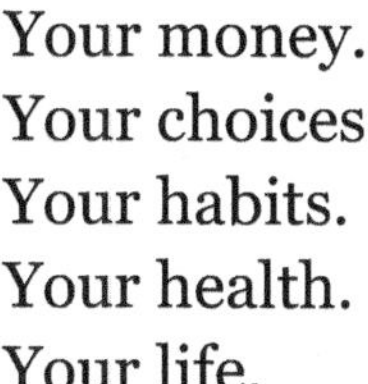

Your money.
Your choices.
Your habits.
Your health.
Your life.

It's on you.
**No one else** is responsible.

Not because you deserve shame...

...but because you deserve freedom from a false narrative.

## What Really Matters

Money in your bank account doesn't determine your worth.
Possessions don't define your success.

Net worth doesn't equate to self-worth.

Not the car.
Not the drip.
Not the house.
Not the brands.
Not the paycheck.

Not in the end.

What matters are your choices—every single day. Your choices are your story.

They can make you.
They can break you.
They ripple outward—influencing others.

Tiny choices create habits.
Habits create character.
Character creates a life.

Even the smallest choice...what you eat, how you spend, what you say, what you do...can change the trajectory of your entire life.

And this is where money finally gets the demotion it deserves and returns to its proper job description: **servant.**

Money can fund your calling or fund your coping.Money can buy time to be present...or buy distractions to avoid yourself. Money can build a family...or create dismantling dysfunction.

It's not the money.
It's who's holding it—and what they're asking it to do.

# Field Work: Steward's Playbook

### 1) Write a Purpose Line.

"I use money to **X** (serve my family, fuel my calling, create margin to be generous, buy time—not status)."

**Put it where you see it.**

## 2) Build a Runway.

Starter: **$1,000** buffer.

Aim: **3–6 months** basic expenses.

Method: auto weekly transfer to a **separate** high-yield bucket

No heroics—consistency.

## 3) Automate the Virtues.

**Give %** → day you're paid.

**Save/Invest %** → same day (retirement, index funds, etc.).

Automation > willpower.

## 4) Barbell Your Budget.

**Essentials** (roof, food, utilities, transport, health).

**Joy line** (guilt-free fun).

**Future line** (invest/give/sinking funds).

Cut noise, not life.

## 5) Add Friction to Mindless Spending.

Delete cards from impulse sites.

24-hour rule for anything over $100.

One "big rocks" day/month for thoughtful purchases.

## 6) Create Sinking Funds.
Mini-buckets: car, gifts, travel, health, house.

$X auto each month.

Emergencies become **events**, not crises.

## 7) Income is a habit.
Skill-up **1 hour/week**.

Apply to **2** roles/month.

Practice **asking** reps: negotiate bills, salary, rates.

Courage **compounds.**

## 8) Tell the Truth Monthly.
Three lines in a note:
**What happened** (facts).

**What I felt** (fear, envy, anger).

**What I'll do** (one change).

Shame dies where the truth is told.

## 9) Guardrails.
***If*** the credit card isn't paid in full monthly, ***then*** it's frozen.

***If*** I miss 2 months of saving, ***then*** I reduce expenses this month by $X.

***If*** work is killing me, ***then*** I set a six-week job-search sprint.

**10) The Open-Hand Prayer (make it your own).**
***"Lord, this is Yours. Make me faithful and free. Show me where to give, where to save, and where to say enough. Thank you for all you've provide and continue to provide. My faith and trust is in you my Lord. Amen."***

## Wrapping Up

Money is not evil.
Money does not make people evil.

Money is simply a tool created long ago to advance civilization.

The tragedy is when we let it replace humility—and God.

There was once a time when people lived in harmony. They survived through shared resources and shared responsibility—gift economics, reciprocity, contribution.

Only the collective good.
Every soul mattered.

Wealth was measured in balance, not bank accounts.

Privatization.
Hoarding.
Status.
And with it, inequality.

Scripture points us higher in Acts 4:32–35...it's a lot so I grabbed some chunks of each verse. But I implore you to read God's word yourself—in full.

*"...them that believed were of one heart and of one soul...which he possessed was his own...they had all things common...great grace was among them all...Niether was there any among them that lacked...possessors of land and houses sold...laid them down at the apostles feet...distribution was made...according as he had need."*

And yet, somewhere along the way, we forgot.
We let money creep into the center of life and identity and survival.

But the cold hard truth remains:

Money will *never* give you joy.
Money will *never* fill any void inside you.

The rich who cling to it are never satisfied.
The poor who idolize it are never at peace.
The middle class who chase it are always exhausted.

***"He that loveth silver shall not be satisfied with silver; nor he that loveth abundance with increase: this is also vanity."*** (Ecclesiastes 5:10, KJV)

So, fuck money.

# FVCK MONEY

Not in the sense of throwing it away.
In the sense of refusing to let it control you.

Refuse to let it define your value.
Refuse to let it be your god.
Refuse to let it tear apart your covenant relationships.

For the fuck sake of Pete.

Money is a **servant**, not a **master**.
A **resource**, not a **ruler**.

And the day you reclaim that truth is the day you finally step a bit further into freedom.

Please—let go of money being a measurement of your worth.

You are worth infinitely more than any number in a bank account.

God Himself is alive inside you, whether you believe it or not, and that is including every one of His provisions.

If God is your Source and money is just a tool, then here's how you start using the tool...instead of letting it use you.

# Chapter 10

# Fvck The Man

**Ego Alert:** The system will clap while it cages your gifts.

**Vow:** I keep my soul. I build my own table. I do what I want.

# What "The Man" Really Is

When I say **"Fuck The Man,"** I'm not asking you to burn down your employer, hire a hitman, or ghost your team on Monday morning.

I'm naming a **system**.
A script.
A religion dressed in khakis and keeps golf clubs in his car... just in case the CEO needs a fourth.

"The Man" is the worship of safety over purpose.

It's the game that says: **trade your soul for a salary and call it responsible.**

And "The Man" isn't just HR and org charts.

It's the algorithms driving your #fyp on TikTok.
Traditions.
Family programming.

And that bossy voice in your head that whispers:
*"Be small. Stay safe. Don't rock the boat."*

This is where the previous chapter started...

When money is the ***master***, people become ***tools***.
When money is the ***servant***, people become ***free***.

That's what "The Man" is.
Not the person.
The posture.

And if "The Man" is a posture, then **Freedom** is a posture too.

And you can audit it.

**Man Audit**: Write the questions down and answer them.

*Where am I obeying a system I secretly resent?*

*Where am I calling it "responsibility" when it's really fear?*

*What part of me keeps performing for approval—even when no one is watching?*

Then look for the telltale symptoms:

*You feel tired, but it's not from work—it's from betrayal.*

*You keep buying things you don't even like to impress people you don't even trust.*

*You call your gifts "hobbies" because taking them seriously would require courage.*

Here's a tip: **you don't have to quit your job tomorrow.**

But you do have to stop letting your job be your god.

**Start with one rebellious act of integrity:**
Tell the truth (kindly)
Set a boundary (calmly)
Build the side thing (quietly)
Stop apologizing for being called (immediately)

The system survives on your silence.

Your life begins when you stop funding it with your soul.

## The Body Knows What's Up

I tried to make the old game work.

Traffic jams—punch clocks—quotas—but eight months in?

The depression starts creeping back in.
Snoring through blaring alarms.
I begged myself to hear them, and my body just...wouldn't. The noise would just fall on deaf ears.

That wasn't laziness—that was physiology.

Misalignment between what you're doing and what your soul is craving to do triggers stress.

**Chronic misalignment → chronic stress → allostatic load**
(the wear and tear of constantly coping).

Psychology has names for this:
**Cognitive dissonance**: when your behavior is at war with your values, your brain throws sand in the gears—anxiety, irritability, numbness.

**Self-sabotage** is sometimes **self-rescue** in disguise: your body hits the brakes because your soul can't find them.

Burnout lands the same way:
**Exhaustion. Cynicism. Inefficacy.**

Check. Check. Annnnd check.

Zoom out and it's not "weakness."
It's math: When demands outweigh resources—autonomy, support, meaning—the fire dies out.

Your body is the compass: headaches, tight chest, shallow sleep, Sunday dread, Wednesday rage, Friday numb.

You're not **weak.**
You are **wise enough to hurt**.

Scripture has been calling this "slavery" long before we called it "adulting":

***"Stand fast therefore in the liberty wherewith Christ hath made us free, and be not entangled again with the yoke of bondage."*** (Galatians 5:1, KJV)

Slavery isn't just chains.
It's a calendar you don't own.
A clock you watch while juggling tasks for someone else's profit.

"The Man" likes to dress up too.

It's favorite costume?

**Security**.

## The Illusion of Safety

"Corporate family."
The gold watch.
Health insurance.
401(k) match.

Then—restructuring. An email. A closed door.
A banker's box for your desk plant and your collection of personality knick-knacks.

My father would tell you if he were here.

Decades of devotion, tossed around whenever the spreadsheet needed blood.

That's not a cabal of evil people; it's a machine obeying its false god: **the bottom line**.

Scripture Smackdown:

***"The rich rules over the poor, and the borrower is the slave of the lender"*** (Proverbs 22:7, KJV)

Mortgage.
Car loans.
Credit cards.

Any signature can be a shackle if it costs you your mission.

I'm not saying "never buy a house."
I'm saying don't sacrifice your life to worship a roof.
*Most* folks spend more time at work making the money to afford the home they're barely ever in.

Then we have people with the big house and the fancy car but can't afford a couch to sit on.

There's a name for that: **house broke.**

It's real.
Please for the fuck—someone make it make sense.

***"Labour not to be rich; cease from thine own wisdom. Wilt thou set thine eyes upon that which is not? For riches certainly make themselves wings; they fly away as an eagle toward heaven."*** (Proverbs 23:4-5, KJV)

Security without freedom is slavery in a much nicer suit.

Keep your costs light.

Keep your purpose heavy.

Keep your allegiance clear.

## Why The Machine Wins
### (And How Not To Be Its Fuel)

Here's how "The Man" keeps good people stuck:

**Golden handcuffs:** fixed costs rise with income (**lifestyle creep**), so you can't afford to leave misaligned work.

**Status signaling:** you buy to be seen (thanks, Veblen), and the **payment** owns you.

**Debt leverage:** lenders optimize for *their* risk, not your **purpose**. Pre-approval is not a wise life plan; it's a **sales ceiling**.

**Shareholder math:** when shocks take a hit, headcount is a "cost center." The machine preserves **margin**, not your mission.

The trick: the system doesn't need ***you*** to be happy.
It only needs you to be compliant.

Then you're, under the contingency of performance and the bottom line, are you accepted into their "family."

I saw it in the corporate world.

I saw it in the affiliate world.
I see it throughout friends and family.

I pray for them all.

## Prayer & Perspective

*"Lord, free me from the yoke I chose. I pray for all those who fall to the chains and bondage of what may be purposeful to others around them but doesn't serve their soul the way you've asked them to. Amen."*

## The Fisher & The Businessman

A high-powered executive finds a fisherman napping by his boat one sunny afternoon. The executive smirks with pride and wakes the fisherman up.

The exec said, "Why aren't you out catching more fish?"

"I have enough for today," says the fisherman.

"I like to spend my afternoons with my wife, play with my kids, take siestas, and play guitar at night with my friends."

"If you worked harder you could buy a bigger boat, then a fleet. In 15 years you could sell the company, retire rich, and..."

The fisherman put up his hand and stopped him, "And what?"

“Move to a small village, fish a little, nap, play with your kids, and play music with your friends.”

**Mic drop.**

Don’t spend your entire life climbing a ladder that leads back to where your heart already is.

## If You Stay—Lead Differently

Some of you will remain inside organizations.

Good.
And that's fine.
But please don't play small and safe.

**Become** the man or woman worth following.

Design **autonomy**: outcome-based roles, not hour-counting.

Fund **soul recharge**: sabbaticals after five years, *real* PTO.

Pay people *before* shareholders when times are lean.

Practice **open-book** leadership.
Share the numbers.
Share the upside.

Treat humans like image-bearers (Genesis 1:27), not a headcount.

Genuine care → higher retention, creativity, and production. Manipulation spikes compliance; love builds legacy.

You don't have to burn the system down.
You can redeem the part you touch.

## If You Leave—Leave To Build

Don't quit to go get "another job," don't even try to fool yourself with it being "something different."

Quit to **build**.

Not everyone must be a **founder**.

But everyone can be a **builder** of *something*: a service, a product, a movement, a community, a family rhythm not ruled by someone else's calendar.

***"And be not conformed to this world: but ye transformed by the renewing of your mind, that ye may prove what is that good, and acceptable, and perfect, will of God."*** (Romans 12:2, KJV)

## The Mustard Seed

**Tiny + faithful + consistent = inevitable.**

Don't despise a small, or slow, start.

Plant the offer.
Water it.

Let God handle the scale.

Here's another beautiful story of how leadership can be giving *and* charitable...

## Stone Soup

A village had learned to survive by hiding.

Winters were hard; taxes were harder.
So when a dusty traveler limped into the square at dusk, doors clicked shut, and curtains twitched.

The well was there, the firewood was stacked, and yet the square was silent.
He set down a dented iron pot, filled it with well water, and built a small fire.

People watched through cracks...curious, yet guarded. The traveler pulled from his pocket three smooth river stones—polished like moonlight.

He smiled like a man carrying a secret and…plop, plop, plop…dropped them one by one into the pot.

Soon the water rolled to a boil.

"Stone soup," he announced to no one and everyone, "is best in a friendly village."

A latch lifted and an old woman shuffled close, a shawl clenched under her chin.

"Stone soup?" she said. "You're mad."

"Maybe." the traveler grinned, "It just needs…a pinch of salt."

From behind the woman, a boy sprinted home and returned with a crooked little tin of salt. The traveler sprinkled, stirred, tasted. His eyebrows lifted.

"Oh my. If this noble village had a carrot, even one, the color would sing."

A carrot arrived, then two, then a small bundle. Then an onion. A bushel of potatoes.

The baker's apprentice, cheeks dusted white, offered day-old crusts to thicken the broth.

The blacksmith's wife handed over a head of cabbage like a trophy.

A farmer came out with marrow from bone.

The pot began to smell like childhood: sweet, savory, the kind of aroma that makes strangers smile at each other without realizing it

Laughter cracked the air like a thaw.
A fiddler tested a string.

When the soup was ready, the traveler lifted the lid.
Steam rose like prayer.
He fished out the three stones, washed them, and placed them back in his pocket, keepsakes, not ingredients.

People who “had nothing” ate until they were warm and full and softer toward each other than they’d been in years.

Stories were traded.
A quarrel three harvests old was settled with a shrug.
Someone broke out in song and dance.
The village remembered its own abundance.

A child tugged the traveler’s sleeve and said, “Mister, how did the stones make soup?”

The traveler winked.
“They didn’t. *You did.* The stones just helped you remember.”

That’s leadership.
That’s entrepreneurship.

Your offer is the stone.
You don’t need to show up with everything, show up with a pot, a spark, and a clear invitation.

Light the fire.
Name what would make it better.
Let others bring the carrots, bones, and barley.

Don't manipulate; *catalyze*.
Movements are cooked, not conjured.

Scarcity breaks when someone dares to boil water in public.

## Moral Math: "American Dream"

Be honest.

If your mortgage + interest + 30 years of maintenance equals obedience to a job you hate, that house is too expensive regardless of the fucking price or how much you love it. Proverbs again for the win:

***"Better is a little with righteousness than great revenues without right."*** (Proverbs 16:8, KJV)

Live *rich* before you become rich.
But apply it to more than money.

Be rich in time—rich in attention, sleep, community, prayer, health, physical movement...anything that ***adds*** to your life.

When more money arrives, it will serve the richness atop the rock solid foundation of obedience.

## What to Build?

**Productized Service:** fixed-scope, fixed-price outcome.

**Guided Experiences:** teach what you know, coach what you've lived.

**Knowledge Kits:** templates, checklists, walkthroughs.

**Community Membership:** office hours + resources + monthly challenge. (recurring revenue = freedom)

**Cause-Driven Projects:** let prosocial work feed endurance.

***"Whatsoever thy hand findeth to do, do it with thy might; for there is no work, nor device, nor knowledge, nor wisdom, in the grave, whither thou goest."*** (Ecclesiastes 9:10, KJV)

And then there's this truth bomb:

***"A man's gift maketh room for him, and bringeth him before great men."*** (Proverbs 18:16, KJV)

Your gift is a key.
Fucking use it.

Otherwise, you lose it, forget where you "saved it," or end up sticking it in the wrong hole and breaking it off inside the lock.

# If You Lead a Company: Be Worth Following

Give, give, give.

A code of honor for leaders who refuse to be "The Man:"

**Share the Pie:**
If you're going to be like Griswald's boss, don't be surprised if cousin Eddie grabs you on Christmas in your pjs.

Create profit sharing programs or meaningful bonuses tied to real outcomes for your employees.

**Protect Time:**
Real PTO—not as a reward.
One month paid sabbaticals for every 5 years of service.
Do not "reward" rest with a heavier workload afterward.

**Human Compensation:**
Pay a living wage without employees begging.

Create apprenticeship pathways.
Not "up or out." Lattices, not ladders.

Tell the truth fast. Bad news early.
No spin. Be transparent.

Serve Their Future. Pay for courses—even if they *leave you better than they came.* (If you fear that, your culture is already dead.)

This is kingdom-like leadership.

Jesus flips the corporate pyramid beautifully:

***"But it shall not be so among you: but whosoever will be great among you, let him be your minister; And whosoever will be chief among you, let him be your servant. Even as the Son of man came not to be ministered unto, but to minister, and to give his life a ransom for many."*** (Matthew 20:27, KJV)

## A Benediction for Builders

May your work be prayer.

May your pricing be fair.

May your calendar obey your calling.

May your home be a workshop of peace.

May money serve your mission quietly and faithfully.

## The Declaration (Read This Aloud)

**(Feel free to alter this to fit your own belief system.)**

# FVCK THE MAN

*I refuse to be owned.*

*I will not give my soul to safety.*

*I will steward my gifts in the open.*

*I will build what God put in my hands.*

*I will serve people, not idols.*

*I will be generous when I arrive and generous on the way.*

*I will be the person worthy of leading.*

*I will help others do the same.*
*Amen.*

# Field Work: Break the Contract

"The Man" isn't your boss at work.

It's the deal you keep renewing with safety and comfort. Now, you're going to break it—quietly, clearly, and in public—enough to make it real.

## 1) Write:

Write the sentence you've been dodging: **"I keep trading my life for safety when I…"**

Don't spiritualize it.
Don't soften it.
Name the behavior.

Now write one more line:

**"The cost of that trade is…"**

That's your receipt.
Make it the cold, hard, truth. Make it hurt.

## 2) Choose your build:

Answer this in one sentence: **"The thing God put in my hands to build is…"**

Keep it simple.
Not your whole empire.
Just the ***next faithful brick.***

### 3) Take one public step:

Do one of these within 24 hours:

**Send the stone:** text one person: "I'm building ______. Do you know anyone who needs help with ______?"

**Name your offer:** post one raw line (not a launch): "I help ______ with ______."

**Ask for a door:** message one connector: "Could you introduce me to someone in _____? I'm serious about building."

No logo. No website. No perfection.
Just one small movement that proves you're done asking permission.

## Wrapping Up

Yes—

Fuck. The. Man.

But do it kindly, gently, strategically, and with purpose.

Not through rage, but through revelation.

Not by burning bridges.
By building your own roads

Because real rebellion isn't reckless.
It's rooted. It's refined.

It can't be bought, bribed, or broken.

The man" isn't just a person.
It's fear dressed in authority.
It's comfort disguised as security.
It's the lie that says you need permission to live your purpose.

But you don't need permission.
You need conviction.

And when conviction wakes up, control crumbles.

If the enemy can't destroy you, he'll keep you busy—chasing promotions that don't fulfill, measuring yourself by metrics that were never divine.

So choose again (because you still can):

Faith over fear.
Purpose over paycheck.
Obedience over optics.

Jesus flipped tables in the temple not because He hated the system, but because the workers of the system forgot the soul's purpose.

They turned worship into transactions, and He returned those transactions back into transformation.

That's rebellion.
Holy rebellion.

# FVCK THE MAN

When you say "fuck the man," you're not cursing humanity...or your boss...you're cursing the illusion of control.

You're renouncing the false gods of money, clout, and convenience.

You're declaring that your spirit is no longer for sale

If you choose to remain in the system, lead differently.
And if you're not yet a leader, learn to be one.

Flip the pyramid.
Serve first.
Build people before profits.

If you do leave the system, please, build something sacred: a business with backbone and integrity, a mission with meaning, a movement that doesn't just inspire—it equips.

A brand that serves.

So—fuck the man.

Serve the mission.
Build the Kingdom.

If you want a new life, stop feeding the machine with your silence. Build something sacred—one brick at a time.

Even if you fall down—***especially*** if you fall down.

# Chapter 11

# Fvcking Fall Down

**Ego Alert:** The fall isn't the problem. Your pity party is.

**Vow:** I get up. I learn. No drama, no delay. I go again.

# The Flood

On August 20th, 2017, my (then) wife and I became business owners. We opened the doors to a group fitness training facility.

It was our retirement fund.
Our kids' college tuition.
Our future mortgage.

It was, by design, to become our family's livelihood.

The first year was a doozy.
And I mean, we broke lease on our new apartment and the four of us moved into the gym.
That's how much I believed in what we were doing. I know it was hard on my ex but I'm eternally grateful she stuck by me for as long as she did. But a woman can only go so long without her own shower.

Then the fateful day arrived.
It started like nothing.
Just any other day really.
We made it the first year—barely—but the gym *was* growing.

That day after classes I went for a trip to the laundromat.

My body was tired.
My brain was on autopilot.
The black and yellow gym towels spinning in the dryer had me in a daze.

It had started to rain a little while I was there.

But rain is just that right? Rain—no big deal.
Background noise really.

I loaded the towels up and started to make my way back. My ex was putting the kiddos to sleep...or so I thought.

The cars in front of me were creeping inch by inch. I could see the lights at the intersection were flashing red.

Still, no big deal.

Slowly but surely I crept my way through the line.
As I got to the intersection, I could see there were police officers blocking the path.

I look left. Blocked.
I look right. Blocked.

Every road to the gym was shut down.
Inconceivable.
Unacceptable.

The officers were standing in the middle of the intersection rerouting all traffic back the other direction. An officer waves at me and points to make a U-turn.

Nope.

I pull forward—still facing down the road I need to go. Roll my window down and I look beyond the squad cars. Then I saw it.

The road home had converted into a raging river of deadly rapids. A half mile or so worth.

The officer approached my window. The first thing I did was laugh—because sometimes laughter is the only way your brain can hold fear without breaking.

“Well...that’s not supposed to be there.”

“Nope! And I can’t let you through. I mean, look at it. No one is making it through that.”

My brain immediately went into protect mode.

“I gotta get back to my family. I *have* to get back to my family”.

The officer interrupted my thought process, “Where are they?”

It took me a second to catch up before I responded, “In the gym over there on Greenview.”

“Sir, everything from here down is flooded. I cannot let you through. It’s just not safe.”

While he’s blubbering about whatever and his duties (rightfully so). I notice I’m right between the two squad cars...but still twenty or so feet back. And there’s just enough room to fit. Like a running back seeing an open hole in a broken play.

I look at the river. I look at him. I look at the 4-wheel lock button. I look back at him. Back at the river.

By now, he's caught on to what I'm thinking. And like a Hollywood movie moment I said...

"Sir—do you have kids?"

"I do," said like he already knew where I was going with this...

"And so if you were sitting here. And they were down there. With your wife. What would you do?"

He sighed before saying, "I'd do whatever I had to do to get there."

Without a word. I locked the wheels into four and threaded through squad cars.

He put on an Oscar-worthy performance "trying to make me stop." But I could tell he was just doing it—for the record.

Straight into the river against the current.

My mind flashed back to Oregon Trail on the old green-screen computers. Fording rivers with a wagon hoping to make it across.

Except this wasn't a game. And this wasn't fording across a river. This was treading *up* a river.

A half mile—that's 2,640 feet. Or 8.8 football fields.

Fucking *fifty feet* in, the water was pushing up over the hood.

The steering wheel trembled.
My pulse spiked.
I felt actual **Amygdala Hijacking**: fear takes the wheel, flooding your system with adrenaline, shutting down logic.

My brain was no longer thinking of a strategy. It was now thinking about survival of my bloodline—starting with me.

Then it happened.
The Santa Fe lifted.

Once.
Twice.
Three times.
Then a fourth time.

Like my vehicle was on a trampoline.

My stomach lurched each time gravity disappeared. I was now floating backwards, at the mercy of the flood.

I prayed.
For the first time in a long time—I prayed.

And before I could finish—the entire vehicle—as if pressed by an unseen hand—slammed back to the ground.

I had traction again.
(God's hand is mighty and I thank Him every day for His good works.)

I finally got to the gym and parked. I stumbled out of the car, shaking from the adrenaline, realizing how close I'd come to possibly drowning in a metal coffin.

That night baptized me in fear.
But it also baptized me in faith.

***"When thou passest through the waters, I will be with thee; and through the rivers, they shall not overflow thee: when thou calkest through the fire, thou shalt not be burned; neither shall the flame kindle upon thee."*** (Isaiah 43:2, KJV)

Storms don't ask for permission to wash you away.

They will test your faith.

## The Grind Into the Mud

The gym was supposed to be my redemption.

A sanctuary.
A community.

A place to turn sweat—and pain—into legacy, fulfilled dreams, and saving countless souls through the years.

That was the plan at least.
My plan.

***"...Father, if thou be willing, remove this cup from me: nevertheless not my will, but thine, be done."*** (Luke 22:42, KJV)

***"A man's heart deviseth his way: but the LORD directeth his steps."*** (Proverbs 16:9, KJV)

Floods don't give a damn about your business plan.
And frankly, neither does God—Ruler of the Universe.

The water wrecked everything—if not physically, then financially and emotionally.

The next day, I watched a news crew on TV fly right over the gym. The water separated and went around both sides of the building, and converged on the other side. The only building in the business park untouched.

I thought all was good.
I didn't think about the Farmer and his son.

I didn't think maybe.

It didn't take long...
Insurance companies were playing the, "It's not a flood zone," card. Members started to drop like flies—draining their savings and cutting expenses to fix their flood damaged homes.

Once again rent loomed like a guillotine with a blood-thirsty executioner.

Survival got ugly—real quick. Tension in my marriage spiked like a diabetic just ate two too many cookies.

Visits to the food shelf. "Showering" in a Rubbermaid storage bin—cold water and grit—hoping my students wouldn't smell yesterday on me.

It's tough for pride to survive when you're clawing at rock bottom.
Scarcity hijacks the fuck out of the brain.

When survival is the only language your nervous system is speaking, long-term thinking becomes more difficult to access. This is where people experience creative blocks—that can cause even more spiraling.

(I experienced this also while writing this book from time to time.)

It's no wonder I couldn't think straight. It's no coincidence in that droughtful season that dreams felt more like a luxurious fantasy.

***"By humility and the fear of the LORD are riches, and honour, and life."*** (Proverbs 22:4, KJV)

Sometimes God strips you down so far the only helpful choice you have left...

is to look up.

**Notice I said "helpful choice."**

I was clinging on though. My pride decided to discern this flood and loss of members as—God testing me to see how much I wanted this life.

I completely ignored what He was actually telling me. I stubbornly went back to rebuilding memberships as if brute force could outmuscle reality and God's will.

But something was certain: I needed a place to bring the chaos and leave it behind.
A friend of mine suggested Brazilian JiuJitsu.

I thought, "Honesty is what I need and BJJ is fucking honest."

Fuck did I get honesty...but not who I was expecting it to come from.

## The Fight After The Fight

I caught on fast but stayed humble. Within a few weeks I was free rolling with black belts and the coaches talked me into a tournament. I hesitated—I didn't intend for this to become competitive—but I agreed.

November 2018. Milwaukee.

The air was thick with sweat and adrenaline.

# FVCKING FALL DOWN

The line to weigh-in looked like one you'd find outside a department store minutes before the doors open on Black Friday.

I stood in line.
I stood in line some more.

Then I heard it:
"Jonathan Nolan, mat five. Jonathan Nolan, mat five."

"What?! I haven't even weighed in yet. (Fuck, I haven't even ate anything yet)"

My first match ever. Lost by one point. The kind of loss that gnaws at you worse than a blowout because it whispers:

You almost had it. Almost.

I shook my opponent's hand like a man, chin up, already reminding myself I have to get *both* feet hooked for points taking the back.

I walked back to the bleachers and sat down with my team.

But this is where the real fight began.

I remember sitting there with my eyes closed. Working to get my breath and my heart rate back to anything close to resting.

Except it wouldn't.

My chest heaved.
My breath stayed rapid.
My heart kept pounding.

My name got called for my next match.
I didn't even have the energy to say, "No."

I was laying on the bleacher at this point.
I could hear my team trying to alert me to the announcement.
I couldn't even speak.

I was starting to think I had to puke.

I consolidated every ounce of energy I could muster—pushed myself upright and stood. I took a step and nearly collapsed. One of my teammates caught me—keeping me from snowballing down the stairs.

I was able to mutter between breaths "outside."
And that's where they brought me.

Somehow—they got me outside.

I was burning up so I stripped off my gi and used the handrail as a kickstand to hold me up.

False alarm.

The cold must have helped in some way though...because I was now able to say four whole words all at once."Bring me back in."

But that was the limit.
That was all I had in me.

I was now feeling extremely weak, heart still pounding out of my chest, breathing was still rapid and becoming increasingly shallow. They had to help me put my pants back on. And helped me through the door.

(I'm thankful to this day my ex had left to pick the kiddos up; none of them had to watch any of this.)

## The Fall

What went down next was...

well...it was me.

As soon as my teammates got me back through the gym doors. To their description, I became so heavy the three of them couldn't hold me up.

Plop.

I became dead weight.
Completely powerless.

And the last thing I heard before I slipped away was three distinctly different voices in panic:

"Fuck, he's turning purple!"
"He's not breathing!"
"Someone call 911!"

I wasn't asleep.
I was gone.

One moment I'm there.
Then I was somewhere else—still "conscious."

By witness accounts, it took approximately 14 minutes for the paramedics to make it on scene.

The paramedics tried everything for about 30 minutes.

Shocks.
Nitro injections.
Nothing.

Then one medic, having served in Afghanistan, had sudden gut feeling. He hooked me up to a saline bag and gave me another shock or two.

This time.
My heart jumped—for the first time in nearly an hour.

***"My flesh and my heart faileth: but God is the strength of my heart, and my portion for ever."***
(Psalm 73:26, KJV)

I didn't see any of it but my team—

# FVCKING FALL DOWN

They watched me fall further than I ever had.
And watched me come back.

When I opened my eyes, I was laying in the ICU.
My kids and their mother, and standing next to them was a doctor.

Things were said.
I don't remember what.
Back to sleep shortly after that.

I woke up later in another room. Alone.

Still in the dark about what happened here on earth.
Still replaying everything I experienced.
I was trying to convince myself it was just a dream.
But I couldn't shake the vividness of it all.

And there was a major difference between this one and all the other dreams I've ever dreamt.

I could feel it.
The textures.
The warmth of the Sun.
Physics.

It felt...real.

And it scared me in a very particular way.

That feeling when doubt converts to belief...like when you feel a friend lied to you—but you later find they were telling the truth.

I realized the truth...and I was begging to accept the truth. But part of me was still arguing with reality.

Minutes later, a nurse and different doctor walked in. I finally got the answers I was looking for.

**Rhabdomyolysis**.

Rhabdo is when your muscles break down so aggressively it floods the bloodstream.
The byproducts flood your bloodstream, spiking blood potassium levels, poisoning your kidneys, and stopping your heart (Huerta-Alardín, Varon, & Marik, 2005).

It's most commonly seen during IronMan races and crush victims (like the fateful 9/11 attack) and otherwise considered rare—although proving to sometimes be fatal.

That's what happened.
My kidneys failed.
My heart stopped.
Flatlined.

Dead.
Then—Undead.

There's a moment after a disaster where your brain goes weirdly quiet.

Like it can't compute the new reality immediately, so it just... stares. Still rebooting.

That silence isn't strength.
It's a state of shock.

And this is where most people lose the plot: *they treat falling down like a verdict instead of a chapter.*

So if you're in the aftermath—here's your **Post-Fall Protocol**:
**Stabilize:** sleep, food, water, one trusted person. Not solutions—stability.

**Tell the truth:** not the polished version. The real one.

**Extract the lesson:** what did this expose? what did it clarify?

**Choose the next brick:** one small action that proves you're still building.

You don't rebuild a life in a day. You rebuild it brick—by brick—by brick.

Boring—unsexy—but faithful bricks.

Falling down doesn't mean you're finished.

Sometimes it means the old foundation was fraudulent... and God loves you too much to let you keep living on it.

So he test's what you've built with fire.

If it burns down, that's on you.

But His grace doesn't burn you down...no.

He wants to see you rebuild.
He wants to see if you learned.

So He will allow you to rise again through His grace.

## The Phoenix

Every culture tells the same truth:

The fall isn't the end.
It's the forge.

The **Phoenix**—a Greek and Egyptian myth—is a bird that lives, burns, and rises again from its ashes.

Not once.
Over and over and over again.

Death isn't always destructive.
Sometimes it's transformative.

***"For a just man falleth seven times, and riseth up again: but the wicked shall fall into mischief."***
(Proverbs 24:16, KJV)

The Japanese echo it with their own proverb:
*"Nana korobi ya oki."*

Fall seven times, stand up eight.

The number of falls isn't what matters.

It's the rise after the fall.

## Golden Cracks:
## The Japanese Art of Kintsugi

In Japan, when a bowl shatters—

They don't sweep it into the trash.
They don't *try* to hid the cracks with clear epoxy.

They take powdered gold, mix it into lacquer, and carefully fill each fracture.

The repair doesn't erase the break.
It highlights it.
Every crack gleams.

Every flaw becomes an irreplaceable piece of art.

This is *kintsugi*.
Golden joinery.

A broken bowl reborn into something more valuable than it was when it was whole. And yes, the value of the item actually becomes greater than before the brokenness.

Each fracture tells a story of survival.
Each scar becomes a declaration:

*I was broken, but I did not stay broken.*

That isn't a weakness.
That's fucking beauty!

And you—

You are no different.

Your cracks.
The failures.
The betrayals.
The broken heart.

They are not things to hide from the world.
They are not shameful.

Cracks are where the light gets in.
Where God's light and His glory can pour through.

Paul's words here are raw:

***"And he said unto me, My grace is sufficient for thee: for my strength is made perfect in weakness. Mostly gladly therefore will I rather glory in my infirmities, that the power of Christ may rest upon me."*** (2 Corinthians 12:9, KJV)

Kintsugi doesn't pretend the bowl was never broken.
It declares the break was part of the design all along.

Stop covering your scars.
Stop hiding the places you've fallen.

They are the seams where heaven meets earth.

The world may say, "you're damaged goods."

God says, *"you're priceless—because of the cracks."*

God will never abandon you.

## The One Lost Sheep

Jesus told a story about a shepherd with one hundred sheep.

One wandered.

Most people would say, "Forget it. Ninety-nine is enough."

But this shepherd left the ninety-nine in the open country and went after the one until he found it.

And when he did, he lifted it onto his shoulders, called his friends and neighbors, and said:

***"Rejoice with me; for I have found my sheep, which was lost."*** (Luke 15:3–6, KJV)

That's the thing about falling.

You think you're forgotten.
You think you're too far gone.
You think you're all alone.
You think no one's coming.

But God doesn't do math like we do.
He leaves the ninety-nine for the one.

He comes after the fallen.

Falling isn't the end when the Shepherd comes for you.
It's just the beginning.

## The Prodigal Son (Luke 15)

A father had two sons.

One day, the younger son demanded his inheritance early. An outrageous insult, as if wishing his father dead. Yet the father divided the property and gave him his share.

The son packed up and left.
For a time, he lived recklessly.

He squandered the wealth on wild parties, shallow friends, and fleeting pleasures.

He thought this was rising.
But then soon came his fall.

The money ran out.
A famine struck.

The "friends" vanished.

The young man found himself starving and desperate, reduced to feeding pigs.

The ***most degrading*** work imaginable in Jewish culture.

Hungry, filthy, and forgotten, he longed to eat the husks he was tossing to the animals. He had hit rock bottom.

But even in the mud, a thought sparked: *Home.*

He rehearsed his speech:

*"Father, I have sinned against heaven and against you. I am no longer worthy to be called your son; make me like one of your hired servants."*

So he began the long walk back, barefoot, and broken.

Yet while he was still far off, the father saw him.
Compassion overwhelmed him.

He ran to his son, embraced him, kissed him, and called for celebration:

*"Bring the best robe. Put a ring on his hand and sandals on his feet. Kill the fattened calf. For this son of mine was dead and is alive again; he was lost and is found."*

The story is clear: **falling doesn't disqualify you.**

Nor is rising about earning it.

## The Science of Rising Again

Psychologists Tedeschi & Calhoun (2004) called it **post-traumatic growth**. The phenomenon where trauma doesn't just break you, it remakes you.

Survivors of death, or "near-death experiences," report deeper appreciation for life, stronger faith, and resilience forged in fire.

Angela Duckworth (2016) calls it **grit**: passion plus perseverance.

It's not talent that makes people rise.
It's refusal to stay down.

Neuroscience agrees—your brain is adaptable.

**Neuroplasticity** means experiencing a fallback in life rewires the brain for resilience. Every "full send" reshapes your circuitry. You literally become stronger by failing–but this is dependent on the choices you make while facing conflict (Kolb & Gibb, 2014).

# Peter's Denial

Peter swore he'd never leave Jesus.
Hours later, he denied him three times.

The rooster crowed, and Peter broke down (Luke 22:61–62).

That was his fall.
But that wasn't the end.

After Jesus' resurrection, He restored Peter with a task:

***"Feed my lambs…Feed my sheep."***
(John 21:15–17, KJV)

The one who fell became the rock Jesus' church was built on.

Falling doesn't mean you're finished...

Sometimes it's God's way of putting you back on ***His*** path—especially when you seem to think you already know where the fuck you're going.

# Every Rep

What's the lesson?

The flood didn't drown me.
The food shelf didn't end me.

The gym collapse didn't bury me—under ground at least.
Rhabdo didn't kill me—for good.

Even death itself doesn't always get the final word.

Falling is training ground.

***"Wherefore I beseech you that ye would confirm your love toward him. For to this end also did I write, that I might know the proof of you, whether ye be obedient in all things."***
(2 Corinthians 4:8–9, KJV)

Every fall is a rep.
Every collapse is a set.
Every bottom has a top.

The bottom is always a chance at a new foundation.

And to build something that lasts—the foundation needs to be strong as fuck.

# Field Work: The Eight Count Reset

## 1) Name the Floor

Finish this sentence:

**"I fell in: _______."**

Then this sentence:

**"It hurt because: _______."**

No essays. No defending yourself. Just truth.

## 2) Find the Crack—Fill It With Gold

Write these out and answer them:

**What this fall revealed about me:**

**What this fall is asking me to learn:**

**What I refuse to repeat:**

This is your "kintsugi line."Not pretty—honest.

## 3) Choose the Eighth Rise

Pick **one** micro-action you can complete **today** in under 15 minutes. Make it painfully specific:

Send the text.
Pay $10 toward the thing.
Drink water + eat real food.
Walk outside for 8 minutes.
Cancel the self-sabotage commitment.
Schedule the appointment.
Clean one surface.
Write 150 words.

Write it like a contract:
**"Today, I will ______ by ______ (time)."**

## 4) Anchor It

Say this out loud:
**"Falling isn't failure. Staying down is."**

Then add:
**"My next right step is:_________."**

## 5) Proof of Life

Before the timer ends, create a receipt:

Screenshot the message sent.
Photo the cleaned space.

Checkmark on a note.
Voice memo: "I did the thing."

## Wrapping Up

So yeah...fuck it.

Fall down.
Collapse.
Crumble into tiny little pieces.

Get knocked out.
Break. Shatter. Bleed.
Cry until there's nothing left to cry.

(I do not however recommend dying for obvious reasons. Resurrection is a tough gig to schedule twice in one lifetime).

Here's the thing: **falling isn't the end.**

It's the forge.
It's where steel is made stronger.
Where God melts away everything fake until the purest form of you is all that remains.

The floods don't drown you. Sometimes they baptize you.
The fires don't destroy you. Sometimes they refine you.
The failures don't define you. Sometimes they re-wire you.

Every hit, heartbreak, betrayal, every moment of burnout...it all becomes divine pressure—pressing you into your purpose.

Because here's a secret the world won't tell you:
Every strong soul you admire was first a shattered one.
Every warrior was once a weeper.
Every saint had seasons of sin.
Every prophet had a pit they fell into.

It's not a sign you're weak.
It's proof that you're human in the battle arena of life.

And that arena is where faith stops being just theory and becomes blood, sweat, and tears. Where belief stops being cute and becomes costly. Where you lose the illusion that you had it all figured out.

That's where I met God.
He had me get up with bloody knees and blazing eyes.
He had me get up when everyone else quit watching.
He had me get up when the applause stopped and the loneliness laughed.
He had me get up because something inside me refuses to die yet.

Call it grit.
Call it grace.
Call it SISU—that Finnish word for the resilience found in the deepest parts of the soul.

Fall seven times.
Stand up eight.

Falling isn't failure.
Staying down is.

## FVCKING FALL DOWN

Rise up, spit the blood out, wipe your mouth, and smile.
Not as who you were, but who you were forged into.

Because God's greatest miracles aren't in the avoiding.

They're in the rising.

Jesus didn't skip the cross; He conquered it.
The tomb wasn't a mistake; it was the setup for the third day.

So fall.
Fall hard.
Fall ugly.
Fall with style if you can—but fall the fuck down.

And when you hit the floor and the world says, "See, they're done," you'll rise with fire in your eyes and a smirk on your lips and say: **"Not today."**

Because fuck falling down? No.
Fuck *staying* down.

You're training your brain to **believe in you**—so you have the balls to *fucking go for it.*

# Chapter 12

# Fvck'n Go For It

**Ego Alert:** "Someday" is like mold on cheese. Cut it off and the rest is still edible.

**Vow:** I move now—regardless of circumstances.

# Let's Fucking Go

This is the chapter where everything we've talked about stops being just theory and comes to life.

So let's pull it all out of the clouds and put it into actual life—where "going for it" felt nothing like a highlight reel.

Because I was fucking terrified.

Terrified to join the military.
Terrified to go to college.
Terrified to become a husband.
Terrified to become a dad.
Terrified to move to Madison and open a business.
Terrified to get divorced.
Terrified to move back to Minnesota.
Terrified to go into the woods alone for two weeks.
Terrified of being hurt again and again.
Terrified of losing.
Terrified of failing.
Terrified of succeeding.

What?
Yeah, there was already an entire chapter on fear.
This is one of those teacher moments where I repeat something to drill it deeper into your brain—and your soul.

Because guess what: **fear doesn't disappear.**

It shows up even more ***when you're called***.
When you step into your purpose.

Fear is what your nervous system does when your near-future gets bigger than your current identity and comfort zone.

Fear will always be lurking.

It was there any time I was winning.
I don't think it ever goes away.
And I'm not going to insult you with the idea that you can magically shoo it away.

The goal isn't to wait until fear disappears. The goal is to get it done while fear keeps running its fucking mouth.

***"Have I not commanded thee? Be strong and courageous; be not afraid, neither be thou dismayed: for the LORD thy God is with thee whithersoever thou goest."*** (Joshua 1:9, KJV)

Notice what it ***doesn't*** say.
It doesn't say you'll never feel fear.

He—God—is telling you you're not alone in facing fear.
So don't let it scare you away.
It says you need to be strong and courageous.
You wouldn't need those without anything to be afraid of.

My kids know it as, "Feel the fear and do it anyway."

That verse happens to be on the cover of the journal I first wrote this very book in.
I saw it every time I was moved to write.
And before the pen hit the paper I read that verse.

Do you think because I went into writing this gut-wrenching book with fearless motivation?

Do you think it faded as I continued to write?

There was some level of fear present from day one...honestly I couldn't tell you exactly what it is I'm afraid of.

Nonetheless—the feeeeeeling is there.

Do you think now that this book is on the shelf—fear will just magically silence itself from my life?

Fat fucking chance...I know evil all too well.

Publishing this will be the second wave—I mean—I already got heat about the book before I even started to type it out.

So stop waiting for fear to leave and start requiring it to come with you—quietly.

**Make a "Go For It Contract"**:

*"I will take one action within 24 hours. I will tell one person the truth so secrecy can't rot it. I will accept that embarrassment is not death."*

Or whatever works for you.

Because going for it isn't a vibe.

It's a decision you keep making while your stomach somersaults like it's auditioning for Cirque du Soleil.

If you're waiting to feel "ready," you'll die holding the blueprint.

Ready is not a feeling.
Ready is a practice.
So yes—be afraid. And do it anyway.

Let fear ride shotgun while Spirit drives.

That's what courage actually looks like in real life: sweaty hands, steady steps, and a holy "watch me."

Courage is never the absence of fear.
Courage is the repeated act of saying:

*Fuck it. Let's go.*

## Regret vs. Risk

We already know what people talk about near the end.

They don't talk about what they did.
They talk about what they didn't do.

The regrets.
The unlived dreams.
The shots they never took.

That's why when I say *Fuck'n Go For It,* I don't mean throw yourself out of an airplane without a parachute.

I mean step into the life you already know you're called to live.

Create.
Risk.
Build.
Sing.
Dance.
Write.
Lead.
Love—like you mean it.

Pursue your passions.

Jesus dropped the mic on this topic in the Parable of the Talents (Matthew 25:14–30)—a personal favorite.

Three servants are given different amounts of money by their master.

Two invest and double their money.
One buries it in the ground out of fear.

When the master returns, he praises the first two.

*"Well done, good and faithful servant"*

and condemns the last one for wasting what he was given.

Fear buried the gift.
Faith multiplied it.

And that's the choice in front of you.

## Don't Chase. Attract.

When you're going for it, don't fucking chase after it.
It doesn't work out of desperation, starvation, or begging the world to pick you.

Chasing smells like panic.

Attraction looks different.
Attraction ***is*** different.

Attraction happens when you're aligned with your purpose—when you're so rooted in who you are, and what you were made to do, that opportunities start finding you.

***"Commit thy way unto the LORD; trust also in him; and he shall bring it to pass."*** (Psalm 37:5, KJV)

**Translation:** Commit. Trust. Move.

Then watch things start happening ***without*** you ***trying*** to force every outcome.

## The Marketplace of Excuses

Let's get real—as if we haven't been already.

For every single excuse you've ever given, there's a dozen ways to shut it down.

Science calls one version of this **cognitive reframing**: flipping the script on your own bullshit excuses so you stop treating them like they're a diagnosis—when really it's just your nervous system throwing a tantrum in the cereal aisle (Beck, 2011).

Fear says: *I can't.*
Faith says: *God is with me.*
Science says: *Your brain is literally built to adapt.*

So quit selling yourself excuses like a cheap vendor at a flea market.

Drop the "I can'ts."

Start hunting the question that changes everything:

"How the fuck can I?"

## Be Real. Be Adaptable. Be Grateful.

**Be adaptable:**
Life isn't about rigid control—it's pivoting.
Think 2020. Uffda.

**Be consistent:**
Even when you don't want to.
Discipline beats motivation every single fucking time.

**Be grateful:**
Gratitude practices are strongly linked with improved well-being and resilience (Emmons & McCullough, 2003).

Complaining never changes a damn thing—but gratitude builds a stronger mind.

## Authenticity Is Everything

I don't believe in faking anything until you make it to whatever.

First of all—make it to what?

Don't fake anything.
People can smell fake from a mile away.

You can't manipulate your way into real success—at least not the kind that doesn't rot your soul.

The right people for your life will love you when you show up as your raw, weird, one-of-a-kind, and authentic self.

***"For do I now persuade men, or God? or do I seek to please men? for if I yet pleased men, I should not be the servant of Christ."*** (Galatians 1:10, KJV)

The right people for your life won't ask—or require—you to wear a mask. A persona mask...not the 2020 ones.

Show up raw.
Show up weird.

Show up you.

## Forgive and Keep Moving

Shit happens.
You will fuck up.
People will fuck up.

Don't be the one to point fingers.
Don't lose your shit—or at least keep it safe.

Create a harmless outlet if, or when, rage is boiling.
Focus on solutions.

Forgive.
Move forward.

If you want to rebuild—do it.
If the other doesn't even if you do—respect it and walk away.

Bitterness doesn't protect your future.

It puts taxes on it.

## Falling on Your Ass

**It's going to happen.** **SEE CHAPTER ELEVEN**

## Childlike Belief

Remember when you were a kid and you actually believed you could be anything?

That wasn't stupidity.
That was pure, unpolluted faith.

Jesus said it like this:

***"Verily I say unto you, Except ye be converted, and become as little children, ye shall not enter into the kingdom of heaven."*** (Matthew 18:3, KJV)

Kids dream fearlessly.

Adults bury their dreams under the excuses of a false security blanket, call it being "responsible," and label it maturity.

The kingdom belongs to the ones who dare to believe again.

For the fuck sake of Pete—let your inner child out of its cage.

## Go For It Anyway

What do you have to lose by going for it?

Sure, you might fail.
You might lose some shit.
But you can always get material shit back.

And you'll gain wisdom, perspective, strength, and maybe even a victory that changes your whole life.

Let me ask you a darker question:

What do you gain by not going for it?

I know one thing: **regret**.

And regret will eat the fucking life out of you.

Waiting until conditions are perfect, and you'll likely never make a move.

# Field Work:
# The "Do It Scared" Show

## Write your Fear Sentence:

"I'm scared to ______ because ______."

## Write your Regret Sentence:

"If I don't do it, I'll regret ______."

## Pick one "talent rep" you can do today:

One email, one call, one page, one post, one application, one walk, one payment, one draft.

One of something. Just one.

## Set a deadline:

"I do it by ______."

## Create a receipt:

Screenshot, photo, checkmark.

Proof beats mood.

# Wrapping Up

Stop the victim bullshit.
Stop worshiping your pain like it's holy.
Stop rehearsing your wounds like they're your identity.
Stop calling yourself broken when you were built for greatness.

Quit shrinking yourself because you shine too bright.
Quit giving your doubt a microphone.
Quit building altars for your excuses.
Quit telling yourself you can't.

You're not damaged.
You're ***developing.***

Every thought telling you you're too late, too dumb, too poor, too tired, too hurt—is a lie.
It's all a fucking lie.

You've believed it for long enough.
Your life is worth living fully.
Your dreams are worth chasing—not someday...

Right fucking *now*.

**Today.**

Your pain has already paid the price of admission.

God is with you—not just when you're winning, but when you're bleeding.

# FVCK'N GO FOR IT

Not just when you're praising, but when you're pacing the floor at 3 a.m. asking, "Why me?"

He was there then.
He's here now.

So whatever it is your big, beautiful, fucking heart desires—if it's good, if it's true, if it's rooted in love and not harm, if it calls you higher and not lower—

Then *fuck'n go for it.*

Because this one life is all you have right now.

No redo.
No "restart" button.
No "Save Game" and come back later.
(And no: Up, Up, Down, Down, Left, Right, Left, Right, B, A Start in this life. That would be pretty sick though.)

The clock is ticking.
So take the shot.

Write the book.
Launch the business.
Tell her you love her.
Forgive the one who didn't apologize.
Start the band.
Plant the tree.
Buy the ticket.
Take the road trip.
Build the tiny house.

Feed the hungry.
Pray for your enemies.

Smile again. Risk again.
Believe again.

Because faith without movement is dead.
*D*reams without discipline are hallucinations.

It's not enough to say you believe.
You've got to *build.*

You've got to *move your feet in the direction of your prayers.*

Because your purpose doesn't start when fear ends.
It starts when obedience begins.

**Live it loud. Live it brave. Live it redeemed.**

And when it's all said and done—when the dust settles,
and your story echoes through eternity—let heaven say:

***"That one...they didn't waste a single drop of it."***

# Ascensus Manifesto

## The Dawn and the Ruins

Morning doesn't always arrive with sunlight.

Sometimes it seeps in through the clouds, the fog, maybe even some smoke.

The first light of a new life is the aching grief after the fall.
The silence after everything you thought would save you finally collapses.

The ruins hum with memory, and for a while that hum sounds like failure.

But if you listen closer, you can hear it shifting—stone to seed, wreckage to rhythm. That's where the rebuilding begins.

The truth is simple and savage: every calling for something higher begins with collapse of something else. And every resurrection starts in the rubble—the broken foundation of what was.

God never builds on foundations He didn't pour; let Him clear the lot.
The tearing down you cursed was the excavation you prayed for.

You wanted peace; He offered purpose.

You asked for comfort; He gave you comfort, but purpose didn't *feel* comfortable. Especially for others.

God's idea of comfort is usually different than your idea of comfort.

You've seen what happens when fear drives and faith rides shotgun.
You've watched the emotions crown themselves kings.
You've buried pieces of yourself under expectations you didn't agree to carry.

Now the smoke is thinning, and through it you finally see the blueprint etched across the bones of your own chest.

It reads: ***Rebuild here.***

This is where *Ascensus* begins.

Not up there in the clouds—down here, ankle-deep in the ashes of everything that didn't last.
The climb starts in the crater.

The mountain grows beneath your feet once you decide to rise.

Fucking look around.
The world you once knew is gone.

# FVCK IT

Not the illusion you thought it was—the real one. And the world you were made for is waiting.
The tools are already in your hands: truth, faith, grit, grace.

The same hands that once clenched in fear now gracefully grip the hammer. And every swing, every word, every breath becomes a prayer of sanctification.

You were not meant to stay buried under yesterday's debris. The darkness of the night wasn't punishment; it was preparation.

Shadows are proof light still exists somewhere, even if you can't see it yet. And light always keeps its promises.

The ruins hum again—louder now. Not with grief, but with potential.

Every broken beam, every shattered dream, every "fuck it" you've ever spoken becomes part of the music of rebirth.

You realize falling wasn't the ending act.
It was the drum roll before the rise.

So stand.
Even if your knees shake.
Even if the dust burns your throat.

Stand. The fuck. Up.
Because the ground under you is holy now.

This is resurrection soil.
This is where God meets you—not as a distant deity, but as a builder with calloused hands.

The dawn isn't a pretty color anymore; it's a decision. It's the quiet "yes" you whisper to yourself when *everything* else in you wants to quit. It's the courage to move before you *feel* ready.

(Psst—your soul is ***always*** ready to fucking move.)

It's the sacred profanity of surrender: *fuck it...let's build.*

## The Fire and the Forge

The result of fire will always look like destruction to what can't survive it.

But to the soul, it's a standard operation procedure.

Flame is the oldest language of renewal; it devours what no longer serves and leaves only the elements that endure.

And you don't choose the fire.
You answer to it.

The forge is not a place of comfort.
It's not meant to be.

It's the place where identity softens, where metal screams, where molecules are rearranged.

Heat reveals composition.
Pressure reveals purpose.

At first, you tried to run from it. Everyone does.
Then you blame the devil, and the timing, and the people who disappointed you.

But then you realize: maybe this isn't Hell.

Maybe this is Heaven in work clothes.
God doesn't always whisper...sometimes He just welds.

When the flames closed in around your fears, everything inside you resisted.

Old stories.
Old guilt stapled to those stories.

The need to please everyone.
The addiction to bring comfort to the uncomfortable.

They all screamed for oxygen.
But every scream was a lie burning to ashes.

And somewhere between the sparks, you saw your reflection in the molten metal. Not the brittle version of you that cracked under judgment—the real one. The alloy of grace and grit that refuses to break.

That's when the truth hit: ***refinement is mercy.***

The same heat you once thought could consume you whole is also the heat that completes you.

The fire isn't here to punish; it's here to purify.

You remembered every time you said "fuck fear," every time you chose motion over paralysis—and you felt those declarations harden into muscle.

Discipline replaced doubt.
Devotion replaced despair.

The fire didn't change who you were; it revealed who you've been all along.

You can't outsource this stage. No mentor, no miracle, no medication can substitute for personal combustion.

The forge is solitary because identity is sacred. It's where God hands you back your own spine and says: *"Now—stand."*

When you step out—smoke still in your lungs—you realize you're lighter.

The unnecessary turned to soot.
The weight you thought was yours to carry isn't on your shoulders anymore.

What remained was pure substance: **Faith that can't be faked, courage that can't be copied and pasted.**

And as the first cool breeze kisses the new steel of your soul, you find a new understanding:
The same fire that terrified you became your teacher.
The same pain that tried to end you became proof that you cannot be ended.

You are the instrument now—forged, tempered, alive.

And the next time the world hands you a flame, you'll smile.
Because you know now what it means.

It means it's time to level up again.

## The Climb and the Crown

When the fire goes quiet, there's always a hush.

A stillness so deep it feels eerie.
You look around and realize the landscape has changed.
The forge is behind you.

Now?
The mountain ahead.

The air smells like iron and rain.
Everything in you aches, but it's a clean ache—the kind that makes you feel like you're alive. Like the first big stretch in the morning after getting out of bed.

It's time to climb.

It doesn't start with a drum roll.
It starts with a single step.
Boots in ash. Knees wobble.
A heart that still remembers how close it came to quitting.

But the mountain doesn't care about your trembling.
It only answers to motion.

The path twists–narrow and cruel–carved by no one other than who once believed what you now believe: higher is holy.

Each ledge demands something different: Courage on one turn. Grit on another. The enthusiasm somewhere near the middle.

You pay in pieces with each step you take—
but the view pays you back.

Up here—the air thins and the noise of the world dies out.

You start to hear what silence really sounds like: now you can hear the quiet voice that's been whispering "yes" throughout every chapter.

It never shouted.
It never begged.
It only waited for altitude—because a lot of truth can't be heard down in the valley.

They're tuned for thinner air.

You remember the lessons in your stack: how expectations crush; fear misdirects; emotion can bend but aren't great in the lead; falling taught you how to fly; the forge made you fireproof.

Every scar adjusts the compass.
Every scar says: **Keep going.**

Halfway up, doubt returns wearing new clothes.
It looks like fatigue.
It sounds like logic.
It says, "You've done enough. Sit here."

But you know its voice now.
You've traded too many dreams for comfort before.
So you lean into the climb, whispering the creed that got you this far: **"Faith over feeling, purpose over pain."**

As the slope sharpens, you notice what's behind you—whole landscapes you never knew you'd outgrow.

Old versions of yourself stare up from below: the fearful one, the bitter one, the sad one, the victim, the enraged, the one who mistook chaos for calling.

You nod to them. They nod back.
They're not enemies anymore; they're proof.

The higher you go, the simpler life becomes.
Less to carry.
Less to prove.
More sky. More soul.

And with every inhale, you understand a little bit more:
Ascent isn't about escaping the earth.
It's about remembering that heaven never left it.

When you finally reach the crown.
The raw, wind-cut summit.
You don't throw your arms up in triumph.
You fall to your knees.

Because the view isn't conquest; it's clarity.
But maybe throw your arms up.

From here, you can see the pattern—the holy geometry of your own story.

Every loss linked to a new lesson.
Every detour by design.
Every "fuck it" a doorway you had to walk through.

And you realize the crown was never gold.

It was gravity reversed.
The weight you carried transformed into light.
You wear it quietly now—unseen, unmistakable.

This is Ascensus: not escape—**elevation**.
Not running from the world, but rising within it.

The climb doesn't end here; it expands here.

The summit becomes the sky.

# The Rising and the Commission

The mountain never gives you permission to stay on top.
It nods once—a silent blessing—then points you back down.

Because revelation that stays private will rot.
The view was never meant to be owned; it's meant to be shared.

So you rise—shoulders square, lungs full of thin air and thick gratitude—and start working your way back down to the rest of the world.

To prepare for your next ascent.

Everything looks different now.
The valley isn't smaller, it's sacred.
The people who doubted you. The ones who left.
Even the versions of you that crawled through darkness.

Each of them is part of the terrain that pushed you up here—to this point.

Bless them without saying a word.
Forgiveness becomes gravity reversed.

You can finally move freely again.

This is the beginning of leadership—the quiet kind.
Not the roar of the ego, but the hum of integrity.

You walk among those still wandering and they feel it with you having to say a word.

Not perfection.
Presence.

The kind of presence that makes people stop you and say, ***"You really own your space."***

You don't preach the climb; you live it.
You build small and quiet—in ordinary places: morning coffee, tired hands, with laughter that won't quit.

You teach without trying because wholeness is contagious.
Transformation that ripples outward by simple proximity.

You start to see how every "fuck it" was really a prayer in disguise:
fuck fear…let courage speak;
fuck expectation…let purpose breathe;
fuck failure…let faith rise.

Each defiance was devotion.
Each wound became an instruction manual for healing.

And now it's your turn to hand out the tools.

You tell them, "The blueprint isn't in my book. It's in your blood."

You tell them, "The same God that lit my fire is whispering in yours."

You tell them, "You don't need a stage. You need a shovel."

Because this movement isn't about worshiping the builder; it's about awakening the builders in everyone else.

The Ascensus spirit doesn't create followers.
That's not even part of the mission.

Fuck numbers.

The Ascensus movement creates founders.

And the commission is simple: **Build something holy from whatever is in front of you.**

If it's words—write.
If it's timber—raise walls.
If it's people—love them into wholeness.
If it's silence—fill it with prayer

You don't wait for the fear to leave anymore—you've learned to bring it along.

You don't chase the light—you've learned to carry it.

Every forward step is faithful worship.
Every act of courage is in communion

Down in the valley, you'll sweat again.
You'll doubt again.
You'll stumble and curse and maybe fall another seven times.

But now you know the secret encoded into every fall:
**Resurrection isn't an event. It's a habit.**

That's what it means to rise.
Not once. Not twice. Forever.

To make every breath you take proof the tomb is still empty.

## The Manifesto of Light

Light doesn't crash in.

It grows—glows outwardly—one breath, one heartbeat, one brave decision at a time.

You awake one morning and realize you're no longer rebuilding.

You're living inside the house you prayed for.
It creaks. It's perfectly imperfect.
It's yours, and the Spirit moved in

Grace isn't a spotlight. It's a sunrise.
It doesn't blind; it reveals.

It exposes the sacred in ordinary things: calloused hands, unpaid dreams, second chances.

You look around and see God in the details—the sawdust, the sweat, the blood.

The calm before the storm—the silence after.

This is the real miracle: not that you survived, but that you can still love.

After everything—your heart beats with the sweetness of honey.

Forgiveness tastes like freedom now—not surrender.
You've stopped begging for doors to open because now—you are the door.

Light teaches differently than fire.

Fire yells; light whispers.
Fire demands sacrifice; light invites presence.

You need both—one to forge you, one to guide you.

Now the world waits—not for your perfection, but for your presence.

Every day you wake up, you are proof that resurrection isn't mythology; it's methodology.

The Ascensus movement isn't an organization—it's a source of oxygen for the weary.

It's the breath you just took.
It's the "fuck it" that turned into faith.
It's the choice to build instead of burn.

So this is your manifesto (feel free to customize this for yourself):

**Live unafraid of falling; you've learned how to rise.**

**Speak truth even when your voice shakes; silence has cost you enough.**

**Love recklessly; it's the only kind that heals.**

**Create relentlessly; beauty is rebellion.**

**Serve quietly; humility is the loudest sermon.**

**Rest without guilt; peace is productivity for the soul.**

And when the world tells you to shrink,
remember the forge,
remember the climb,
remember the light of dawn that came through the smoke.

Smile. Stand tall.
Whisper the two words that started it all:

**Fuck it.**

Not as defiance, but as devotion.
Not rebellion against God, but rebellion against every lie that kept you from Him.

It's the sacred shorthand for surrender.
The heartbeat of freedom.

You were built to rise.
Built to forgive.
Built to create.

Built to love.
Built to ascend

Keep rising.
Keep loving until love is all that's left.

And when you reach the next mountain—there will always be another mountain—don't curse the climb.
Welcome it—because every ascent carves new space for more grace.

And when the final sunset comes, when breath runs thin and the horizon blurs, you'll know: you didn't waste a single heartbeat hiding.

You lived.
You gave.
You built.
You burned bright.

You'll exhale one last time and grin at the mystery waiting beyond the veil. "Fuck it," you'll whisper.

"I already lived in full light."

And heaven will echo back,

**"Welcome home, builder."**

# THE CONTINUATION

This is not the end.

This is the breath before the next build.

What you just read was not written to decorate a shelf, collect dust, and make you feel briefly inspired before life drags you right back into the same old loops. This was written to wake you up.

To hand you a sledgehammer.
To drag truth into the open and call your soul back to life.

The demolition is done.
Now comes the reconstruction.

Now comes the part where you stop nodding at the page and start answering the call on your life.

Because revelation that never leaves the page will rot there.

Truth that never reaches your habits, your work, your relationships, your faith, your discipline, your calling, and your courage eventually turns into spiritual clutter. Nice language. Dead motion. Decorative conviction. And this book was never written to make you sound deep. It was written to make you move.

That is why Ascensus exists.

Ascensus is the living ecosystem beyond this book. Not a brand in the hollow internet sense. Not a vanity project. Not a stage with my name in bigger letters than the mission. This is infrastructure for builders. A path for the people who felt something crack open while reading this and know damn well they cannot go back to sleep now.

Because this movement is not about creating followers.

It is about awakening founders.

Builders.

Leaders.

Writers.

Mothers.

Fathers.

Artists.

Misfits.

Faith-driven rebels.

People who are done performing and ready to build something holy with what God already put in their hands.

So no, this book is not the finish line.

It is the match.
Next is the fire.

Keep climbing.

The commission continues.

# ASCENSUS ARCHITECTURE

The book is the spark.

The ecosystem is the structure around the flame.

What began in these pages continues through the work, tools, spaces, gatherings, and teachings being built through Ascensus. Every part is designed to move this message from idea to embodiment.

From inner stirring to outer construction.
From "that hit me" to "my life is changing."

## The Workbook

***Blueprint for a Soul: Field Work for Fvck It***

This is where the words leave the page and enter your hands.

The workbook is built for application.

Reflection. Journaling. Practices. Exercises. Field work. Real-life integration.

Not vague inspiration.
Not "circle how you feel and hope for the best."

Actual work. Actual movement. Actual excavation.
This is where readers stop admiring truth and start practicing it.

*Exclusively on Amazon.*

## The Course

### *The First Ascent*

Some people need to read it.
Others need to hear it.
Others need to walk through it step by step.

The course takes the core framework of this book and expands it into guided teaching, deeper explanation, implementation, and lived discipline.

Chapter by chapter.
Brick by brick.
No hype.
No guru nonsense.

Just honest teaching for people serious about rebuilding from the inside out.

Grab the whole bundle.
Or cherry pick from individual chapters for your immediate needs.

You can see the details at: *www.ascensuspath/courses*

## The Podcast / Audio Teachings

### *The Ascensus Path Podcast*

For the days when you do not need another scrolling session.

You need a voice in your ear reminding you who the hell you are.

The podcast and audio teachings exist to carry this message into your commute, your workout, your prayer walk, your late-night unraveling, your morning rebuild, and every ordinary space where truth needs to land in real time.

Stories.
Teachings.
Conversations.
Fire.
Depth.

Maybe a few table flips.
Depends on the day.

Have a listen at: *www.ascensuspath.com/podcast*

## The Community

### *The Forge*

Few are successful climbing alone. And no one should have to unless its God's command. Hey Moses!

The community exists for builders who are tired of shrinking, pretending, and trying to carry everything in silence. It is a place for connection, sharpening, accountability, encouragement, truth, prayer, and shared ascent.

Not performance.
Not curated masks.
Not "let's all pretend we're crushing it."

Real people. Real growth. Real (re)building.

Find it at: *www.ascensuspath.com/forge*

## Retreats & Live One Day Gatherings

### ***Ascensus Path Retreats***

Some things need space. Some things need stillness.

Some things need a room full of people who are all brave enough to stop each other at the same time.

Retreats and live gatherings are where this work steps out of private reading and into embodied experience.

Teaching.
Worship.
Reflection.
Rest.
Honesty.
Renewal.
Reconstruction.

The kind of moments that leave you different because your soul finally had room to breathe.

Opportunity is knocking: *www.ascensuspath.com/retreats*

## Speaking & Workshops

This message was never meant to sit quietly in one binding.

It is meant to enter rooms.

Churches.
Men's groups.
Women's groups.
Leadership gatherings.
Conferences.
Podcasts.
Schools.
Sports teams.
Organizations.
Workshops.

If you'd like to inquire about booking opportunities you can email: ***media@ascensuspath.com***

## Future Books, Tools, and Resources

This is not a one-book universe.

More is coming.

More books.
More field guides.
More tools.
More teaching.

More resources for people ready to rebuild their lives with honesty, courage, discipline, and faith.

Because the mission is not to create one moment.

It is to build a body of work people can live inside.

# START HERE

You made it this far and it's worth asking yourself why.

Maybe curiosity.
Maybe hunger.
Maybe pain.

Maybe the quiet realization that you are done surviving a life you were actually called to build.

Whatever brought you here, honor it. Do not close this book and tell yourself you will come back “someday.”

Someday is one of hell’s favorite lies.

Start now.

There you’ll find the next step into the Ascensus ecosystem, including:

The workbook.
The course.
Podcast and other recordings.
Retreats and live gatherings.

Community access.
Speaking and workshop information.

Future books, tools, and resources.

And anything else related...

Here's a free gift just for you.

**SCAN TO START**

*or go to ascensuspath.com/start*

You do not need to have your whole life figured out.

You just need to stop abandoning the part of you that knows you were made for more.

One honest step can change a life.

Take it.

# ACKNOWLEDGMENTS

First—**God**. In Jesus' name I give you all my gratitude for the path You laid in front of me.

The One who met me in the rubble—every time. Who corrected me when I was loud and wrong. Who held me when I was quiet and feeling broken, and kept showing up even when I wasn't showing up for Him. And for redirecting me when I get distracted by Your creations.

**Jesus**—I thank You for Your mercy that does not flinch. For Your grace that continues to be gifted—especially when it wasn't earned. The kind of love you give freely that doesn't only forgive, but rebuilds.

**Holy Ghost**—Thank You as well for the nudges, confirming pokes, the conviction, the peace with resistance, the comfort, and the strength that didn't make sense on paper but somehow lifted me up daily. Even carried me entirely some days.

**To my children:** You both are my WHY. You two are the reason I'm still here. How I learned to rise without applause. You have this way of pulling my head out of the sand when I seem to be buried too deep. You both have this radar I cannot fly low enough under when I'm having a rough day with my own dark clouds—as if you can see the clouds yourself. Thank you for always applying your grounding touch in those times. Thank you for your patience when I struggle to make the most of our time together. Thank you for always being you truest selves and keeping my debate skills sharp. But most of all...

Thank you for always shaping the clouds into funny characters and helping me laugh through the tears.

I appreciate the level of understanding the three of us have.You two understand me, my purpose, and what it means for the world more so than most adults.I understand you both have had to make sacrifices in your own lives for me to get to this point. There's no amount of gratitude—or words—I could express to cover what your choices have meant to me. I know the distance between us most days is tough.

Remember: nothing in this life lasts forever.

Yet—the love you continue to express toward me is so unconditional and wholesome—I'll be honest. There are days I don't feel worthy or deserving to be your father—terrible actually. A terrible and selfish father.

What I think of most: I cannot lose you—because I love you both so very much.

So much my heart expands like a balloon when we're together. Thank you—thank you, thank you, thank you. For who you are and who I see you becoming. For challenging me to become a better father—a better human.

**To my mother:** Thank you for believing in me just enough when believing in me was expensive. For standing in the storm when I told you I didn't want you to.

For the sacrifices, the unseen labor, and the strength it takes to keep moving when life starts swinging.Our story has chapters I won't write here out of respect—but I honor what you carried when no one else would—including the parts of you that helped shape the better parts of me.

Thank you for having enough love that stayed. For the prayers you prayed when I didn't even know I needed them. For your support, the meals, the listening, and the occasional reality check when my stubbornness creeps from below the surface.

I want you to know I—nor God—see any of my failures or setbacks in my life as a reflection of you as a mother. I would be a fool to ever think I could ask for anyone better.

**To my Dad:** I don't know how to thank someone who isn't here to read it for himself.

I miss you in the ways that sneak up on me—the random moments, the quiet victories, the hard days when I catch myself reaching for your voice like it's still on the other end of the line.

There are parts of me you built that I didn't recognize until you were gone. The grit. The stubborn get-up. The parts that keep moving when life is heavy and nobody's clapping.

I'm still becoming the man I wish you could see—still learning how to carry love without armor, how to be steady, how to lead with my hands open instead of my fists tight. And sometimes I swear I feel you near—not in a spooky way...in a *strength* way. Like something in me stands up a little straighter when I say your name in my head.

If heaven has front-row seats, I hope you've seen what I've survived. I hope you've seen what I'm building. And I hope you know this: your legacy didn't die with you. It's breathing in my choices. It's showing up in how I father, how I fight, how I forgive, how I rebuild.

This book carries some of that.
It carries a piece of you.

Thank you for that.

I love you, Dad. I'll see you again.

**To my coaches and teammates**—all of you over the years—especially the ones who've watched me break and come back.

Thank you for being in the grind with me, sharing the discipline, the accountability, and the kind of brotherhood that doesn't care about my excuses. You taught me that character isn't what you say you are—it's what you do when you're tired, embarrassed, and still expected to show up.

**To my friends:** who read the drafts, listened to my rants, sat with me in seasons of chaos, and never asked me to shrink to be palatable: thank you. Thank you for giving me space to be a human, and messy, and real—with no judgment.

You reminded me that healing isn't a straight line—it's a decision you make again and again. You reminded me how grief is just as unique of a process as we are unique in ourselves. Your support and presence in my life will forever be held with gentleness, gratitude, and care.

**To my readers**—yes, you:

Thank you for trusting me with your time and your attention. I don't take that lightly.

If any page in this book felt like it reached into your chest and grabbed something honest, that's not an accident. That's God doing what He does—turning pain into purpose and ashes into new foundations.

If you're still in the middle of it, still carrying the weight, still trying to figure out how to rise again—hear me: you're not disqualified. You're not behind. You're not too far gone.

You're in the process.
And the process is holy.

So take what helps.
Leave what doesn't.

And build something real.

With gratitude,
**Jonathan**

# Bibliography

A-Tjak, J. G. L., Davis, M. L., Morina, N., Powers, M. B., Smits, J. A. J., & Emmelkamp, P. M. G. (2015). A meta-analysis of the efficacy of acceptance and commitment therapy (ACT) for anxiety and depression. Behaviour Research and Therapy, 77, 30–44. https://doi.org/10.1016/j.brat.2015.12.007

Aesop. (2002). Aesop's fables (L. Gibbs, Trans.). Oxford University Press.

Alter, A. L. (2017). Irresistible: The rise of addictive technology and the business of keeping us hooked. Penguin Press.

Amabile, T. M., & Kramer, S. J. (2011a). The power of small wins. Harvard Business Review, 89(5), 70–80.

Amabile, T. M., & Kramer, S. J. (2011b). The progress principle: Using small wins to ignite joy, engagement, and creativity at work. Harvard Business Review Press.

Baumeister, R. F., Bratslavsky, E., Muraven, M., & Tice, D. M. (1998). Ego depletion: Is the active self a limited resource? Journal of Personality and Social Psychology, 74(5), 1252–1265. https://doi.org/10.1037/0022-3514.74.5.1252

Beck, J. S. (2011). Cognitive behavior therapy: Basics and beyond (2nd ed.). Guilford Press.

Berridge, K. C. (2007). The debate over dopamine's role in reward: The case for incentive salience. Psychopharmacology, 191(3), 391–431. https://doi.org/10.1007/s00213-006-0578-x

Brewer, J. A., Worhunsky, P. D., Gray, J. R., Tang, Y.-Y., Weber, J., & Kober, H. (2011). Meditation experience is associated with differences in default mode network activity and connectivity. Proceedings of the National Academy of Sciences of the United States of America, 108(50), 20254–20259. https://doi.org/10.1073/pnas.1112029108

Carhart-Harris, R. L., Muthukumaraswamy, S., Roseman, L., Kaelen, M., Droog, W., Murphy, K., Tagliazucchi, E., Schenberg, E. E., Nest, T., Orban, C., Leech, R., Williams, L. T., Williams, T. M., Bolstridge, M., Sessa, B., McGonigle, J., Sereno, M. I., Nichols, D., Hellyer, P. J., ... Nutt, D. J. (2016). Neural correlates of the LSD experience revealed by multimodal neuroimaging. Proceedings of the National Academy of Sciences of the United States of America, 113(17), 4853–4858. https://doi.org/10.1073/pnas.1518377113

Clear, J. (2018). Atomic habits: An easy & proven way to build good habits & break bad ones. Avery.

Craske, M. G., Treanor, M., Conway, C. C., Zbozinek, T., & Vervliet, B. (2014). Maximizing exposure therapy: An inhibitory learning approach. Behaviour Research and Therapy, 58, 10–23. https://doi.org/10.1016/j.brat.2014.04.006

Dimidjian, S., Hollon, S. D., Dobson, K. S., Schmaling, K. B., Kohlenberg, R. J., Addis, M. E., Gallop, R., McGlinchey, J. B., Markley, D. K., Gollan, J. K., Atkins, D. C., Dunner, D. L., & Jacobson, N. S. (2006). Randomized trial of behavioral activation, cognitive therapy, and antidepressant medication in the acute treatment of adults with major depression. Journal of Consulting and Clinical Psychology, 74(4), 658–670. https://doi.org/10.1037/0022-006X.74.4.658

Dweck, C. S. (2006). Mindset: The new psychology of success. Random House.

Fiorillo, C. D., Tobler, P. N., & Schultz, W. (2003). Discrete coding of reward probability and uncertainty by dopamine neurons. Science, 299(5614), 1898–1902. https://doi.org/10.1126/science.1077349

Garrison, K. A., Zeffiro, T. A., Scheinost, D., Constable, R. T., & Brewer, J. A. (2015). Meditation leads to reduced default mode network activity beyond an active task. Cognitive, Affective, & Behavioral Neuroscience, 15, 712–720. https://doi.org/10.3758/s13415-015-0358-3

Graeber, D. (2011). Debt: The first 5,000 years. Melville House.

Griffiths, R. R., Richards, W. A., Johnson, M. W., McCann, U. D., & Jesse, R. (2008). Mystical-type experiences occasioned by psilocybin mediate the attribution of personal meaning and spiritual significance 14 months later.

Journal of Psychopharmacology, 22(6), 621–632. https://doi.org/10.1177/0269881108094300

Hagger, M. S., Wood, C., Stiff, C., & Chatzisarantis, N. L. D. (2010). Ego depletion and the strength model of self-control: A meta-analysis. Psychological Bulletin, 136(4), 495–525. https://doi.org/10.1037/a0019486

Hall, K. D., Ayuketah, A., Brychta, R., Cai, H., Cassimatis, T., Chen, K. Y., Chung, S. T., Costa, E., Courville, A., Darcey, V., Fletcher, L. A., Forde, C. G., Gharib, A. M., Guo, J., Howard, R., Joseph, P. V., McGehee, S., Ouwerkerk, R., Raisinger, K., ... Zhou, M. (2019). Ultra-processed diets cause excess calorie intake and weight gain: An inpatient randomized controlled trial of ad libitum food intake. Cell Metabolism, 30(1), 67–77.e3. https://doi.org/10.1016/j.cmet.2019.05.008

Hofmann, W., Baumeister, R. F., Förster, G., & Vohs, K. D. (2012). Everyday temptations: An experience sampling study of desire, conflict, and self-control. Journal of Personality and Social Psychology, 102(6), 1318–1335. https://doi.org/10.1037/a0026545

Jacobson, N. S., Martell, C. R., & Dimidjian, S. (2001). Behavioral activation treatment for depression: Returning to contextual roots. Clinical Psychology: Science and Practice, 8(3), 255–270. https://doi.org/10.1093/clipsy.8.3.255

Jung, C. G. (1968). Aion: Researches into the phenomenology of the self (R. F. C. Hull, Trans.; 2nd ed., Collected Works of C. G. Jung, Vol. 9, Pt. 2). Princeton University Press. (Original work published 1959)

Killingsworth, M. A., & Gilbert, D. T. (2010). A wandering mind is an unhappy mind. Science, 330(6006), 932. https://doi.org/10.1126/science.1192439

Knutson, B., & Cooper, J. C. (2005). Functional magnetic resonance imaging of reward prediction. Current Opinion in Neurology, 18(4), 411–417. https://doi.org/10.1097/01.wco.0000173463.24758.f6

Kross, E., & Ayduk, O. (2011). Making meaning out of negative experiences by self-distancing. Current Directions in Psychological Science, 20(3), 187–191. https://doi.org/10.1177/0963721411408883

Krumrei-Mancuso, E. J., & Rouse, S. V. (2016). The development and initial validation of the Intellectual Humility Scale. The Journal of Positive Psychology, 11(3), 215–233. https://doi.org/10.1080/17439760.2015.1048818

Lally, P., van Jaarsveld, C. H. M., Potts, H. W. W., & Wardle, J. (2010). How are habits formed: Modelling habit formation in the real world. European Journal of Social Psychology, 40(6), 998–1009. https://doi.org/10.1002/ejsp.674

Montague, P. R., Hyman, S. E., & Cohen, J. D. (2004). Computational roles for dopamine in behavioural control. Nature, 431(7010), 760–767. https://doi.org/10.1038/nature03015

Nour, M. M., Carhart-Harris, R. L., Timmermann, C., Roseman, L., & Nutt, D. (2016). Ego-dissolution and psychedelics: Validation of the Ego-Dissolution Inventory (EDI). Frontiers in Human Neuroscience, 10, 269. https://doi.org/10.3389/fnhum.2016.00269

O'Doherty, J., Dayan, P., Schultz, J., Deichmann, R., Friston, K., & Dolan, R. J. (2003). Temporal difference models and reward-related learning in the human brain. Neuron, 38(2), 329–337. https://doi.org/10.1016/S0896-6273(03)00169-7

Porter, T., Elnakouri, A., Meyers, E. A., Shibayama, T., Jayawickreme, E., & Grossmann, I. (2022). Predictors and consequences of intellectual humility. Nature Reviews Psychology, 1(9), 524–536. https://doi.org/10.1038/s44159-022-00081-9

Rollnick, S., Miller, W. R., & Butler, C. C. (2008). Motivational interviewing in health care: Helping patients change behavior. Guilford Press.

Rotter, J. B. (1966). Generalized expectancies for internal versus external control of reinforcement. Psychological Monographs: General and Applied, 80(1), 1–28. https://doi.org/10.1037/h0092976

Schultz, W. (1997). Dopamine neurons and their role in reward mechanisms. Current Opinion in Neurobiology, 7(2), 191–197. https://doi.org/10.1016/S0959-4388(97)80007-4

Sinclair, S., Beamer, K., Hack, T. F., McClement, S., Raffin Bouchal, S., Chochinov, H. M., & Hagen, N. A. (2017). Sympathy, empathy, and compassion: A grounded theory study of palliative care patients' understandings, experiences, and preferences. Palliative Medicine, 31(5), 437–447. https://doi.org/10.1177/0269216316663499

Smith, A. (2013). *The wealth of nations (A modern abridgement).* **Penguin Classics**. *[Penguin Classics modern abridged edition]*

Sripada, R. K., Kahana, S. Y., & Angstadt, M. (2014). Aberrant reward center response to partner reputation during a trust game predicts outcomes in borderline personality disorder. Biological Psychiatry, 76(10), 830–839. https://doi.org/10.1016/j.biopsych.2014.04.015

Tagliazucchi, E., Carhart-Harris, R., Leech, R., Nutt, D., & Chialvo, D. R. (2014). Enhanced repertoire of brain dynamical states during the psychedelic experience. Scientific Reports, 4, 6369. https://doi.org/10.1038/srep06369

Timmermann, C., Roseman, L., Haridas, S., Rosas, F. E., Luan, L., Kettner, H., Martell, J., Erritzoe, D., Tagliazucchi, E., Pallavicini, C., Girn, M., Alamia, A., Leech, R., Nutt, D. J., & Carhart-Harris, R. L. (2023). Human brain effects of DMT assessed via EEG-fMRI. Proceedings of the National Academy of Sciences of the United States of America, 120(13), e2218949120. https://doi.org/10.1073/pnas.2218949120

Tong, E. M. W., Koh, A. H. Q., & Yuen, A. Y. L. (2019). Awe and human perception: Seeing the big picture increases meaning and prosociality. The Journal of Positive Psychology, 14(2), 156–165. https://doi.org/10.1080/17439760.2017.1388433

Wang, D. D., Li, Y., Afshin, A., Springmann, M., Mozaffarian, D., Stampfer, M. J., Hu, F. B., Murray, C. J. L., & Willett, W. C. (2019). Global improvement in dietary quality could lead to substantial reduction in premature death. The Journal of Nutrition, 149(6), 1065–1074. https://doi.org/10.1093/jn/nxz010

Wegner, D. M. (1994). Ironic processes of mental control. Psychological Review, 101(1), 34–52. https://doi.org/10.1037/0033-295X.101.1.34

White, R. E., Kross, E., & Duckworth, A. L. (2019). Self-distancing from future stressors facilitates adaptive coping. Emotion, 19(4), 623–637. https://doi.org/10.1037/emo0000465

Whitehouse, H., Kavanagh, C. M., & Jong, J. (2019). *The deep history of group identities: The cultural evolution of communities, tribes, and nations.* Current Opinion in Psychology, 26, 80–84.

Wood, W., & Neal, D. T. (2007). A new look at habits and the interface between habits and goals. Psychological Review, 114(4), 843–863. https://doi.org/10.1037/0033-295X.114.4.843

World Health Organization. (2015). Guideline: Sugars intake for adults and children. https://www.who.int/publications/i/item/9789241549028

NOTES

# NOTES

# NOTES

NOTES

www.ingramcontent.com/pod-product-compliance
Lightning Source LLC
LaVergne TN
LVHW010628110826
845149LV00014B/2804

* 9 7 9 8 9 9 5 3 6 2 3 0 2 *